# THE HOUSE
# THAT THOMAS BUILT

Thomas de la Rue, painted by William Troutschold, 1851

# THE HOUSE
# THAT THOMAS BUILT

*The Story of De La Rue*

*By*

LORNA HOUSEMAN

1968

CHATTO & WINDUS

LONDON

Published by
Chatto & Windus Ltd
40 William IV Street
London W.C.2

\*

Clarke, Irwin & Co Ltd
Toronto


SBN 7011 1343 X

Printed in Great Britain by
Westerham Press Ltd
Westerham, Kent

*To*
*the men and women of*
De La Rue
*and for*
A.E.H.

# *Contents*

CONTENTS CONTINUED

# Illustrations

## COLOUR PLATES

# Acknowledgements

MY thanks are due to my father for providing enough material for several books covering the period of De La Rue history 1921–45; Mr Roger Tilley for his patient support and for assistance in researching; the late Mr John Easton for his generosity in placing at my disposal the results of his research into Inland Revenue and Post Office records, as well as other material amassed in five years' work on *The De La Rue History of British and Foreign Postage Stamps* for the Royal Philatelic Society of London; Mr Leslie Newman for his help in the initial stages; Mr Arnold Strange for kindly checking the typescript; Mr E. A. Morrison for helping to disentangle the legal aspects of the firm's affairs; Sir William Arnold, Mr T. F. Priaulx, Mr J. Sheppard and other friends in Guernsey and the Channel Islands for answering innumerable queries; the Rev. Edmund Lister regarding Bishop's Nympton and the Warrens; Mrs Cruwys Morchard, Secretary of the Devon Society; le chef du Service Relations Extérieures, S.A. Formica, Paris for facts of Warren de la Rue's school and academic life; Hambros Bank and the Eagle Star Insurance Company for permission to quote from their archives; Dr Norah Nicholls for details of the Royal Chest Hospital; the Victoria and Albert Museum for permission to reproduce Selous's picture of the Great Exhibition on the dustjacket; last but not least to the de la Rue family, Miss Margaret Müller, and to members of the De La Rue Company, past and present, without whom I would have no tale to tell.

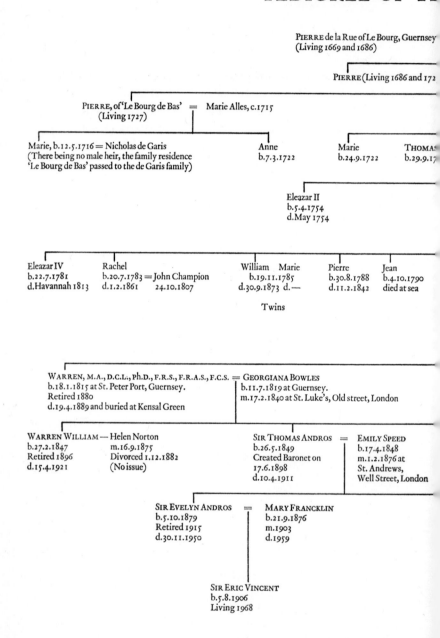

# PEDIGREE OF TH

PIERRE de la Rue of Le Bourg, Guernsey
(Living 1669 and 1686)

PIERRE (Living 1686 and 172

PIERRE, of 'Le Bourg de Bas' = Marie Alles, c.1715
(Living 1727)

Marie, b.12.5.1716 = Nicholas de Garis
(There being no male heir, the family residence
'Le Bourg de Bas' passed to the de Garis family)

Anne
b.7.3.1722

Marie
b.24.9.1722

THOMAS
b.29.9.17

Eleazar II
b.5.4.1754
d. May 1754

Eleazar IV
b.22.7.1781
d.Havannah 1813

Rachel
b.20.7.1783 = John Champion
d.1.2.1861    24.10.1807

William   Marie
b.19.11.1785
d.30.9.1873 d. —

Pierre
b.30.8.1788
d.11.2.1842

Jean
b.4.10.1790
died at sea

Twins

WARREN, M.A., D.C.L., Ph.D., F.R.S., F.R.A.S., F.C.S. = GEORGIANA BOWLES
b.18.1.1815 at St. Peter Port, Guernsey.
Retired 1880
d.19.4.1889 and buried at Kensal Green

b.11.7.1819 at Guernsey.
m.17.2.1840 at St. Luke's, Old street, London

WARREN WILLIAM — Helen Norton
b.27.2.1847
Retired 1896
d.15.4.1921

m.16.9.1875
Divorced 1.12.1882
(No issue)

SIR THOMAS ANDROS =
b.26.5.1849
Created Baronet on
17.6.1898
d.10.4.1911

EMILY SPEED
b.17.4.1848
m.1.2.1876 at
St. Andrews,
Well Street, London

SIR EVELYN ANDROS =
b.5.10.1879
Retired 1915
d.30.11.1950

MARY FRANCKLIN
b.21.9.1876
m.1903
d.1959

SIR ERIC VINCENT
b.5.8.1906
Living 1968

# LA RUE FAMILY

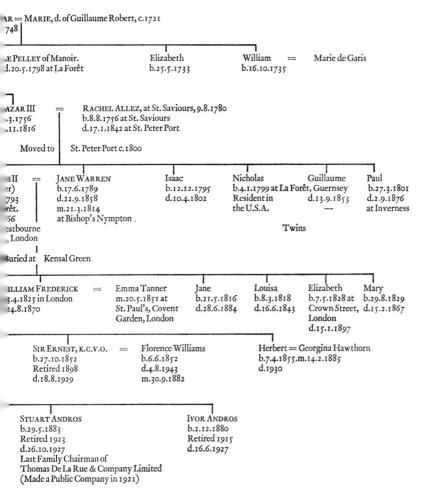

ALLES of Le Casrouge, Guernsey. c.1664

ALLEZ, daughter of Francois of La Carriere

AR = MARIE, d. of Guillaume Robert, c.1721
748

E PELLEY of Manoir.          Elizabeth          William    =    Marie de Garis
d.20.5.1798 at La Forêt        b.25.5.1733       b.16.10.1735

AZAR III    =    RACHEL ALLEZ, at St. Saviours, 9.8.1780
.3.1756            b.8.8.1756 at St. Saviours
.11.1816          d.17.1.1842 at St. Peter Port

Moved to    St. Peter Port c.1800

S II    =    JANE WARREN         Isaac              Nicholas                   Guillaume        Paul
r)            b.17.6.1789          b.12.12.1795       b.4.1.1799 at La Forêt, Guernsey   b.27.3.1801
793           d.22.9.1858          d.10.4.1802        Resident in      d.13.9.1853    d.2.9.1876
rêt.          m.21.3.1814                             the U.S.A.          —           at Inverness
56            at Bishop's Nympton .
estbourne                                                            Twins
, London

Buried at    Kensal Green

ILLIAM FREDERICK    =    Emma Tanner        Jane          Louisa        Elizabeth          Mary
3.4.1825 in London        m.20.5.1851 at     b.21.5.1816   b.8.3.1818    b.7.5.1828 at      b.29.8.1829
24.8.1870                 St. Paul's, Covent d.28.6.1884   d.16.6.1843   Crown Street,      d.15.2.1867
                         Garden, London                                 London
                                                                        d.15.1.1897

        SIR ERNEST, K.C.V.O.    =    Florence Williams        Herbert = Georgina Hawthorn
        b.27.10.1852                 b.6.6.1852               b.7.4.1855.m.14.2.1885
        Retired 1898                 d.4.8.1943               d.1930
        d.18.8.1929                  m.30.9.1882

STUART ANDROS                    IVOR ANDROS
b.29.5.1883                      b.2.12.1880
Retired 1923                    Retired 1915
d.26.10.1927                    d.16.6.1927
Last Family Chairman of
Thomas De La Rue & Company Limited
(Made a Public Company in 1921)

# THE HOUSE
# THAT THOMAS BUILT

# CHAPTER I

## *Guernsey small-holdings*

WITH however wild a surmise the parents of the infant Thomas de la Rue looked at their new offspring it is unlikely that they saw any future for him. That their seventh child, born in a small, already overcrowded, Guernsey farmhouse should become one of the Island's famous men, that he himself, let alone his children and grandchildren, should hob-nob with the great of England and be on speaking terms with Royalty was beyond the bounds of probability. In their rural seclusion they did not dream that he would found a London company, one destined to become a household word in different corners of the world. Besides, Eleazar and Rachel de la Rue had little time in which to dream.

*     *     *

Somehow prosperity had always passed the de la Rues by. The Iles Anglo-Normandes were traditionally well situated for privateering. Guernsey, particularly, was an ideal base from which to sail forth and capture prizes. During the Wars of the Spanish Succession Guernseymen brought their prowess in this activity to such perfection that results were felt as far afield as Bilbao and Dunkirk. No ship along the Biscay Coast was safe. The little Channel Islands were making an appreciable difference to the French economy. 'Ces mauvais Corsaires infectent toute cette coste cy', wrote the Commissaire de Marines at Nantes in April, 1708. The promise of rewards was so tempting that even amateurs could not resist indulging on the side.

Ninety years later Channel Islanders were eagerly anticipating a protracted struggle between the French and the English. Their hopes were realized. But while other Guernseymen grew fat on privateering proceeds, Eleazar de la Rue allowed his financial position to grow steadily weaker as his family grew steadily larger. In the end he had nine children to support. Thomas came into the world the year that King Louis XVI left it via the guillotine – in 1793.

*　　*　　*

The hamlet where Thomas de la Rue was born, and where he spent his short childhood years before being put to work, was Le Bourg in the parish of La Forêt, the second smallest parish in the Island. In 1800 the population of Guernsey was 16,155, excluding 'sailors in His Majesty's service, privateers and merchant vessels', but the entire population of La Forêt totalled only 552 persons.

De la Rues had lived at La Forêt for generations. They were first mentioned there in the time of Elizabeth I in 1581, when an 'extente' of property was drawn up: 'Collas de la Rue, Collas son of Collas, Collas son of Massy, Martin de Mouillpied in right of his wife daughter of Collas de la Rue and the heirs of John de la Rue' were all listed as being of La Forêt.

Whereas earlier de la Rues were elders of La Forêt church and members of the parish douzaine or council, Eleazar took no part in parish affairs. Any signs of enterprise among the children of Eleazar and Rachel seem to have been inherited from the maternal line, the Allez-Andros families. In 1607 a complaint was made to the Royal Commissioners that Martha Allez was 'unlawfully carrying away the stones of the fort or castle of La Corbière under pretext of purchase'. More recently and respectably, Rachel's grandfather, Charles Andros, was King's Sheriff, a proud fact which may have been responsible for all male de la Rues of the line in Edwardian times being named Andros. Rachel's parents, the Allez's, owned a manor-type house at St Saviours. Their social and financial standing was superior to Eleazar's.

2

His own farmhouse at Le Bourg was near the only village shop. Together with 46 vergées and 32 perches of land, it had been handed down through the de la Rue family for the last century. A vergée being 2/5ths of an acre, 46 of them would represent a small-holding today, but the register shows the de la Rue estate to have been of average size for the eighteenth century.

An inventory of another Guernsey farmhouse, similar to Le Bourg, and with the same acreage, was taken around the year of Thomas's birth. Its details furnish a picture of his boyhood. Apart from 'Prayerbooks' and a 'Book of Psalms', the only books were one Bible 'very old with brass clasps', two liturgies, an 'ancient book of Sermons' and a book entitled *Emmanuel* 'in very poor condition'. The few refinements consisted of six Delft plates and a Delft mug, five pillowslips of fine linen, a pair of silver buckles and a silver ring with a stone. Items of clothing were mostly 'coarse' or 'much worn'. There was the best feather bed, (weight 73 lbs), one set of bedhangings, one bedspread and one pair of sheets, plus, in Shakespearian tradition, 'the second best bed' with bolster and two pillows (weight 58 lbs), 'an old mousetrap' and 'last year's manure which is in the yard'. Fishermen's baskets indicate how diet and income were supplemented; 'seaweed sickles' and 'the remainder of the seaweed and other fuel' reveal how the family kept warm. Items 218 and 232 were simply 'the hay'. The chief livestock were a grey mare, a red mare, two milking cows, 'the big bullock' and 'the bullock with white markings'. There were two bushels of broad beans, five earthenware honey jars, apples both stacked and pulped, and a lot of assorted cider barrels.

\*     \*     \*

In order to widen the road at La Forêt the original house at Le Bourg was pulled down by the Germans during the last war. Senior inhabitants of the village remember it well. They recall that it gave straight on to the road, and had two rooms up and two down; on the left, as one entered, was the much-used kitchenlivingroom, and on the right the little-used parlour, both with stone floors; a lean-to wash-house was built on at the side, and pig-sties adjoined the back of the house. Eleven de la Rues slept in the two upstairs rooms. In winter they tramped in out of the mud into conditions which, if cramped and fuggy, were at least warm since the walls were thick. The ceilings were low – too low to suspend lamps overhead, say the seniors of La Forêt. In summer the small windows let in little air, but not far away was the lane to Petit Bot Bay to wander down when farmyard chores were done.

*     *     *

By 1802, if Eleazar had been capable of taking an appraising look at his finances, he would have seen ruin staring him in the face. While he muddled on blindly, the burden of feeding eleven mouths was falling squarely on Rachel. Her husband might be content to scratch out an existence on his land but she could no longer afford to disregard their plight; there was no future for their regiment of children on the farm. Something had to be done, and Rachel would have to be the one to do it. Eleazar had shown how ineffective he was in business matters. He was incapable of selling even the smallest plot of ground and advertised the same two little meadows for sale month after month for a whole year in the *Gazette de l'Île de Guernsey* until they must have been the joke of La Forêt.

Eventually the de la Rues managed to sell the farmhouse, and with the proceeds they bought a house in the centre of St Peter Port, the island's capital. It was half way up a steep street called Le Bordage. Auguste Vacquerie listed the salient features of early nineteenth century St Peter Port as being 'a Gothic church; old narrow, irregular, fantastic and amusing streets, intercepted by climbing and stumbling flights of steps; the houses piled on top of one another so that they all got a glimpse of the sea; a tiny harbour crowded with shipping with the yard arms in constant danger of smashing the windows of the quay'.

4

Like Dickens's Mr Micawber, the de la Rues were briefly wealthy on the minute profit they had made by changing houses. At the same time they attempted to make some kind of provision for their children. It was arranged that two of the older boys, William (twin of Marie) and Jean should go to sea. Pierre was put to work in a shop and eventually had one of his own. But the eldest, Eleazar IV, as unsuccessful as his father, flitted to Havana owing 'Henry de Garis and others' the sum of £336. Circumstances beyond his control may have contributed to his undoing, since his unpaid bills included debts to doctors and surgeons.

As yet no decision had been taken about the future of Thomas, who was showing signs of precosity. In St Peter Port, at any rate, there were more openings to choose from than in La Forêt. There was one which had the advantage of being close by: lower down the street lived Joseph Antoine Chevalier, a master printer, who needed an apprentice. A few months after the move from La Forêt, on 1st March 1803, Thomas de la Rue became that apprentice. He was nine years old. In a surprisingly good hand, appreciably firmer than his father's, he put his signature to a document which he himself had written. It contained only one crossing out; first he put himself down as being 'agé de dix' which in fact he nearly was, as his tenth birthday was only three weeks away, but to be on the right side of the law or Mr Chevalier, he changed it to 'agé d'onze'.

The document stated that Eleazar 'allowed the hire' of his said son to Mr J. A. Chevalier for the term of seven years, during which time Thomas, in the customary language of apprenticeship papers, promised to serve his Master faithfully. In return Mr Chevalier was to teach 'all and as much of the art of printing which the said apprentice is able to learn'. For the first two years he was to work for nothing. In his third year he would receive the sum of two shillings a week, three shillings in his fourth, rising in his final year to six shillings. He was to be given one day a week off.

Mr Chevalier's main production was the *Gazette de l'Île de Guernsey*, the first printed newspaper on the island. Occasionally it carried advertisements on its own behalf; one, for apprentices, stressed that the position gave 'a good opportunity to further education'. It was by grasping this opportunity that Thomas de la Rue received the major part of his schooling. Produced in French and English, but running at the most to a thousand copies, the *Gazette* could only support one experienced journeyman. The apprentices were, of necessity, boys of all-work, and as such Thomas gained a thorough knowledge of printing.

*　　*　　*

Meanwhile his father's affairs were going from bad to worse. Compared with the two-up-and-two-down accommodation at La Forêt, the town house was palatial. Besides two kitchens, a washhouse, two attics, a cellar and 'un petit édifice en derrière', it had six main rooms. Soon Eleazar found it was too big. Isaac, his eighth child, had died shortly after the move. His eldest girl was engaged to marry a solid citizen some years her senior – the John Champion who stood witness to Thomas's apprenticeship papers. Finding a *dot* for her further depleted the current funds. William and Jean were now both at sea. Eleazar's town house was already proving to have been an expensive mistake.

In addition to borrowing from Rachel's respectable relations the only course was to try to dispose of Le Bordage to its best advantage and buy a smaller house. Finding one vacant in the Rue de la Fontaine Eleazar promptly bought it. But typically he then discovered that he was unable to sell the house in Le Bordage. Now he was stuck with both. Trying all permutations he advertised desperately, offering the Bordage house either for sale as an outright purchase, or to rent unfurnished, or to let as apartments 'avec toutes les commodités'. There were no bidders and the advertisements continued until Eleazar died.

The ratesbooks confirm the downward spiral of Eleazar's finances. In the year 1801 the records in the Constable's Office in St Peter Port show that he paid £3 tax. His prospective son-in-law, John Champion, paid £46 10s tax for the same year. Two years later Eleazar was paying a pound less tax, whereas John Champion was paying more. By 1810 Eleazar was assessed at only 15 quarters of *rente* (equal to £300 capital), the lowest amount taxable. Any Guernseyman who had less was considered to be a mere peasant.

John Champion bought his wife, Rachel, a shop opposite the pumps in the market place where she sold sugar, candles, 'soap by the cwt or quarter cwt', good cheese and 'plusieurs autres articles' at low prices. Inspired by his daughter's success Eleazar tried running a shop from his new house in the Rue de la Fontaine, where he advertised 'd'excellent vinaigre de vin blanc à vendre'. But however excellent the vinegar, his fortunes were beyond repair. By the last year of his life, Eleazar was too poor even to appear on the list of taxpayers.

\*      \*      \*

In 1811 Thomas's term of service to Mr Chevalier was completed. Conveniently forgetful of his promise to keep his master's trade secrets, he immediately started looking for a job where he could use them to advantage. There were not many printing posts to choose from in St Peter Port. Apart from his ex-master's paper, the only established rivals were the *Mercury* and the *Star*.

While searching for work Thomas met a man called Tom Greenslade, who had emigrated from Bishop's Nympton, a village in Devon. With a lot of other Englishmen he had come to take advantage of the booming prosperity in Guernsey – doubtless having heard that the Battle of Trafalgar had successfully put paid to any French designs on the Channel Islands. The sort of man to appeal to Thomas, he was adventurous, enthusiastic, willing to try any project, including running the Guernsey lottery which, by a questionable coincidence, he succeeded in winning himself.

Thomas started to drop by Greenslade's shop, a general stores in the Pollet, to discuss an attractive idea. The population of Guernsey, swollen with prosperity and the presence of a hefty garrison, could, the two men decided, support another newspaper – a 'journal politique and litteraire'. Greenslade contracted to take eighteen-year old Thomas on as editor. What decided Greenslade upon giving young de la Rue this chance was not so much any special genius Thomas had for the art of printing, as the more persuasive fact that he guaranteed to get the subscribers.

Thomas said he spent the next year successfully recruiting 'the names of a great many of the most respectable persons in this Island' to subscribe to the new paper. The society of Guernsey was sharply divided; there were the 'Soixante' top families, and a further 'Quarante'. Being tradesmen the de la Rues were not in either, but some of their Allez-Andros relations were included, a circumstance of which Thomas was free to avail himself in the course of his first piece of salesmanship.

It is said locally that he tried to climb into the Soixante-Quarante sets and that because he did not succeed he turned his back on Guernsey. Subsequent evidence does not support this theory. At no stage of his life, except perhaps towards the end of it, and then for pressing personal reasons, did he give a hint of caring whether or not he was considered a tradesman. Even after he had become prosperous he was the first to take off his jacket in moments of urgency – carefully charging for his overtime. Thomas's interest in the island's upper class was professional. In Guernsey, like everywhere else in 1811, it was the higher echelons of society which constituted the reading public. Business beckoned Thomas in their direction.

A source of potential subscribers lay in the assorted clubs which began to flourish in St Peter Port at the end of the eighteenth century. Elisha Dobrée, the Guernsey diarist, belonged to at least three – the ladies had their own – the 'Sociable', the 'Humdrum' and the 'Brilliant'. It was also in these clubs that the main gossip of the Island was exchanged; for a journalist the frequenting of them was an absolute necessity. In addition they were the centres of card playing, which had recently become enormously popular in Guernsey. While passing through the club rooms the sight of so many pasteboards on the card-tables of St Peter Port cannot have escaped young de la Rue.

By September 1812, Thomas had collected enough subscribers, and Tom Greenslade enough wherewithal, to launch the new paper. On the 26th the first edition of the *Publiciste* appeared. It was to be a weekly, on sale 'tous les samedis chez T. Greenslade au bas du Pollet et chez T. De La Rue au haut de la rue de la Fontaine'. Old Eleazar's house was at last serving a constructive purpose. In turn he profited from his son's venture by obtaining some free advertising, offering his Bordage house for sale in the first four consecutive issues.

*   *   *

Although originally Tom Greenslade and Thomas felt themselves to be kindred spirits a longer association proved their similarity of temperament to be too close for comfort. Both men had fiery tempers. Within three months they had quarrelled bitterly. Their paper ran jointly for only thirteen editions. The last number to bear both their names appeared on 19th December.

Then Thomas walked out. Before Greenslade could produce his editorial in the fourteenth *Publiciste* the following Saturday, young de la Rue had forestalled him by writing, printing and circulating a notice in French and English.

TO THE PUBLIC

'I have made engagements to the public and I
shall fulfil them, but am not one of those who say:
It matters not, my fortune is made . . .'

9

he begins. After this thinly veiled reference to his erstwhile partner his grammar deserts him. 'Reasons are powerful' he writes, then forgetting in his heat to finish the sentence, continues: 'is impertinent to the Reader, force me to discontinue partnership with Mr Greenslade; all common interest ceases between us from this day . . .' adding with self-righteous indignation: 'but the firm contracts we made to the public are not less binding in my eyes'.

He protested that in order to continue the paper himself he would have gone and 'hired a press and all the requisites, but it was impossible'. It was impossible for lack not only of funds but of time. A nineteen year old boy, even one as persuasive as Thomas, could not hope to raise the backing of an entirely new paper almost overnight. Where between one Saturday and the next could he find enough people to guarantee his support? He had done well enough to get his handbill out in a couple of days, let alone publish a whole journal on his own. Ingenuously he apologises for not having done the latter. He announces his immediate intention of setting off for London and not coming back before he has furnished himself with a 'compleat set of types far superior' to Greenslade's and 'with paper of a similar high quality'.

A strange certainty permits him to announce that he will be in a position to continue his *own* journal from the 6th February next, i.e. in just over one month's time. Only a definite promise of support could have enabled him to deliver this announcement so firmly. From what quarter did the offer come? Not from his penniless father, nor from the Allez-Andros families, who in all probability were bored stiff by the demands of their poor relations. His sister's marriage, however, had recently brought a hitherto untapped relative in John Champion. Captain Champion was making money fast. His income had increased to such an extent that he was now being assessed at 390 quarters a year, as opposed to Eleazar's 15 quarters. He was shortly to move to Haute Ville, where the well-to-do of St Peter Port had their mansions. The Champion resources were more than equal to Thomas's needs, and he lost no time in availing himself of them.

\*　　\*　　\*

After Greenslade had digested the contents of Thomas's circular letter battle between them commenced. In the editorial of the *Publiciste* Greenslade, maddened by de la Rue's insinuation that he could not care less about his public, swore that he supported his large family by 'labour and honest dealings'. Moreover, he protested, in exchange for half the profits de la Rue had signed an agreement to manage the working part of the *Publiciste* for five years. Here our sympathies cannot but incline to the older man. Thomas undoubtedly failed to honour his contract.

Mr Greenslade himself had not only stuck to his side of the bargain, he maintained; he had exceeded it by providing Thomas with extra help 'from a second person'. Imagine his astonishment when his young partner suddenly told him that unless this assistance was established on a permanent basis he could not 'continue the paper longer than Christmas'! Since it was already mid-December this was hardly fair warning from someone who had entered upon a five year contract. The *Publiciste* was only a couple of months old, and Thomas had not yet given it a chance to get over its teething problems. When he stormed off he thought he would be irreplaceable. In this, as Mr Greenslade hastened to point out with understandable satisfaction, he was wrong. Another editor, Mr Sansabre, was able to step into Thomas's empty shoes immediately, and the *Publiciste* would continue as before.

\*　　\*　　\*

Ironically it was Greenslade who was involved in Thomas's meeting with his future wife, Jane Warren. She came from the same Devonshire village as Greenslade, and was in fact his relation by marriage. Bishop's Nympton was so isolated that intermarriages were frequent in its small community and in the course of time there had been several alliances between Warrens and Green-slades.

Jane Warren's family was still more numerous than Thomas's, and in so far as he owned no property of his own, her father was less well endowed even than Eleazar. Jane's mother had a little money from the Eastmond family mills in the adjacent parishes of Mariansleigh and Meshaw – but not enough to guarantee local suitors for all her daughters. By staying at home the Warren girls had but indifferent prospects of marriage, or of employment. To obtain either it would be necessary to venture further afield. The problem was where.

Tom Greenslade mentioned that he had been home visiting in Devonshire. In a village like Bishop's Nympton the return of a native was an event. A vociferous man, as we know him to have been, he was bound to hold forth to his friends and relatives in the old country about his new life in the Channel Islands. A resultant ray of hope could well have lit in father Warren's heart: St Peter Port – a possible place to find positions for his girls, nearer and cheaper to get to than London, with the advantage of Cousin Greenslade to keep an eye on them, even to employ them himself, either as assistants in his shops, or as home-helps for Mrs Green-slade and the numerous offspring. In any case Jane was already getting on in years; in her mid-twenties she was of an age to look after herself. As Thomas had no opportunity to be in England, their meeting must have taken place in Guernsey before Messrs Greenslade and de la Rue became *incommunicado*.

\* \* \*

Thomas brought out his paper on schedule. On the very day promised, Saturday 6th February 1813, the first issue appeared of the *Miroir Politique*, price 3d. His financial supporters were pre-pared to remain anonymous, and he was named as the sole proprietor. Henceforward he was his own master.

Now that he had a platform of his own he could not wait to use it. In the first number of his *Miroir* he reopened hostilities between himself and Greenslade. 'Désirant du plus sincère de mon coeur d'avoir plus rien de commun avec T. Greenslade' are his opening words. Considering that his *Miroir Politique* is the latest comer on the newspaper scene it is with extraordinary bravado that he provokes the other Guernsey journals: 'Quatre journaux françois! C'est assez, c'est beaucoup; c'est trop peut-être pour cette île'.

His competitors did not care for this kind of talk. The *Mercure* and the *Publiciste* promptly attacked him in their columns, and some of his enemies attacked him elsewhere. Just after midnight on the 12th February 'some evil disposed persons' crept along to Thomas's office in the Pollet and 'maliciously threw stones'. The second issue of Thomas's paper was due out the next morning. In those early days he did not have a trained boy to help him, and the entire production depended upon him. His opponents knew very well he would be working late and determined to give him a fright. They only broke one pane of glass, but Thomas was so incensed by their action that he offered the excessive reward of £8 for information leading to the conviction of the offenders.

£8 was infinitely more than he could hope to make from a week's profits. If he achieved the improbable feat of selling a thousand copies of a new journal, that would have brought in £12; he could not have taken more than a pound from a handful of advertisements. Set against the combined sum of £13 the overheads and cost of printing materials, and there is little room left for profit.

Whether he did it intentionally or not, by stirring up conflict Thomas drew attention to himself. For someone not yet of age he was provoking high feelings. This was an atmosphere upon which he proved to thrive. Far from succumbing to Greenslade's threats to ruin him, his paper continued not only to survive but to prosper. After two months Thomas was advertising for additional help, not for a mere child apprentice but for a boy '14 to 15 years old'.

What was more, he announced, in consequence of a great increase in the number of subscriptions, the *Miroir Politique* would shortly appear in fine print on paper 'd'un qualité superieur'. He had ordered all the necessary materials specially. This, together with his reference in the opening number to his 'renouvellé' equipment, confirms the earlier impression that Thomas did not start the *Miroir* with new plant from London, as was his declared intention. He had bought some second-hand, probably overhauled it himself, and waited to see if it would pay off before investing in new equipment.

As a newspaper proprietor it was the form rather than the substance which interested him; the actual print rather than the contents. He strove to produce the *Miroir* in print superior to that of its rivals. Encouraged by favourable reactions to his efforts, Thomas issued a special edition of the Liturgy and the Psalms – the only volumes, together with the Prayerbook and the Bible, to be found in average Guernsey homes. He had already published his intention to produce a Bible in ninety weekly parts illustrated by the engravings of an English artist called Richard Westall. Thomas could go off to Bishop's Nympton to marry Jane Warren in the knowledge that his printing activities were beginning to diversify and progress satisfactorily.

*　　*　　*

After turning off the main coaching road from South Molton the grandiose spire of Bishop's Nympton's parish church is visible for some distance ahead, deluding the traveller into thinking he is about to descend into a town of some size. Having breasted the final hill a glance down reveals thatched cottages clustered on either side of a single street. 'A large village with fertile ground and well watered by rivers' is how a nineteenth century Gazetteer describes it. One might add that the surrounding hills made Bishop's Nympton as inaccessible as if it had been fortified. Because of the size of their family the Warrens had cause to rejoice that the young Guernseyman had taken one daughter off their hands. Twenty-six year old Jane, born in a generation which believed, like Elizabeth Elliot in *Persuasion*, that after her mid-twenties a woman 'felt her approach to the years of danger', also had reason to feel relieved. But what of Thomas, who had not even celebrated his twenty-first birthday and was four years her junior? Why should he want to marry an older woman from an impecunious family in this remote Devonshire village?

The Warren girls had some attraction. For Jane's sister Sarah married twenty-four year old Paul de la Rue, Thomas's younger brother, when she was thirty-one, well over Jane Austen's danger limit. Obviously the two sisters were neither ill favoured nor unaccomplished in the eyes of the de la Rues.

There was also another reason for the de la Rue brothers to marry out of Guernsey. They lived at a time when the island's social conventions were still rigidly adhered to. Wedding outside the appropriate families was frowned upon, and early marriage strongly discouraged; children constituted a source of free labour for their parents. In such matters it was the *mater familias* who had the final word. As Eleazar was his wife's inferior not only in wealth but in health, Rachel's word carried more than usual weight. Whereas Eleazar survived only for another two years, Rachel lived for another twenty. Had Thomas and Paul not chosen outside the island she would have selected their brides for them. 'The young people who broke away from this system', says a Guernsey historian, 'were those who learnt a trade and were adventurous enough to emigrate'. The de la Rue boys did both these things.

\* \* \*

What finally decided Thomas upon emigrating as soon as possible was Eleazar's decision to sell both his houses at once, the one in the rue de la Fontaine as well as the other in the Bordage. It did not take Thomas long to work out that if Eleazar actually achieved a sale his parents would have nowhere to live except with him. He had rented one of the neat hillside villas in Mount Durand, St Peter Port, to bring Jane home to after their marriage. It was the right size for a honeymoon house for them, but not for Eleazar and Rachel too. Moreover if Thomas allowed his parents to move in with them it would be difficult to avoid responsibility for their debts.

*    *    *

As far as Guernsey was concerned the Napoleonic Wars were over. The French ships could no longer be captured for prize money, and the boom was finished. With all the returned soldiers, sailors and privateers there were not enough jobs to go round. Money was short. For a man of any great ambitions the prospects in St Peter Port were unpromising. Early in 1815 Jane gave birth to a son and heir, who was called Warren in honour of her family. If Thomas was thinking of emigrating the time to do so was now before conditions got any worse in the Channel Islands, or his family any larger.

The last issue of the *Miroir Politique* with Thomas as proprietor was dated 18th July 1815. After the 128th issue his brother-in-law, John Champion, took over. The resultant financial settlement gave the young de la Rues some working capital; since Jane was pregnant again the necessity of putting it to immediate use, and making a decision about their future, was urgent. It forced Thomas to go to England to find somewhere to set up a business. His name, however, remained on the list of the Guernsey militia, indicating that he returned to the Channel Islands. In the spring of 1816 Jane gave birth to a daughter, named after her. Thomas could not let his wife make the journey to England unaided with two babies and their household possessions. He would have had to return to accompany them, and also to wind up his affairs in St Peter Port.

In the autumn of 1816 father Eleazar died, and the long-suffering

Champions took in Thomas's mother Rachel for the rest of her life. John Champion bore some feeling against Thomas, possibly because he felt he was deserting his responsibilities by going off to England. He stated his intention of continuing the *Miroir Politique* on his own, and to make it clear that Thomas de la Rue had no further connection with it he took the unusual step of saying in block letters across the top of the front page that he, J. Champion, was the PUBLISHER. The fact that his wife was a de la Rue prevented him from indulging in the verbal fisticuffs which Thomas had exchanged with Greenslade. But had all been well between them, Champion would certainly have mentioned Thomas by name when announcing the change of management. As it was he preserved a stony silence, and Thomas left not only the *Miroir Politique*, but Guernsey, under a family cloud.

*　　*　　*

Two small clues point to the next whereabouts of Thomas de la Rue. The first is a morocco bound notebook which, fortunately for this story, still exists. In it Thomas wrote out in English and in French a collection of recipes for different methods of printing, in addition recording his own experiments and thoughts on a variety of subjects. The earliest entries are undated. Inside the book is the label of the shop where he bought it: Syles of Barnstaple.

The second clue is the circumstance of both Thomas's first London partners being Barnstaple men. It is unlikely that he ran up against them by chance in the City streets. He remained mistrustful of strangers all his life. Presumably they were already known to him – and it was now that he must have made their acquaintance. Barnstaple was only 15 miles down the South Molton road from Bishop's Nympton. After landing in the west of England from St Peter Port, the de la Rues, with two year old Warren and one year old Jane, had to break the journey somewhere. Yet they had no money to spare, and inns were expensive.

Jane's home at Bishop's Nympton was almost *en route*, and however crowded with Warrens, presented somewhere to shelter. Also, after nearly three years' absence in Guernsey, it was natural for the Warrens to wish to see their daughter and their grandchildren before they set off for London.

The society of Bishop's Nympton was limited compared with life in St Peter Port. Thomas was essentially a businessman. He was also impatient. Although he had been brought up on a farm agriculture was not his *métier*: country matters no longer concerned him. When rural talk palled the nearest place of escape was Barnstaple. Thither he clearly repaired. A printer first and last, he would ask after the state of the trade in England. It transpired that the name of the local printers in Barnstaple was Cornish. It was more than coincidence that this was also the name of his first printing partner in London, whom we know to have been a Barnstaple man. Local historians tell us that Cornish is an unusual name in Devonshire.

It was tempting for Thomas to think of setting up at once in his own trade of printing. But as yet he was uncertain of many things in England. With a wife and family to support he must try and check an instinct to gamble. There could be no plunging into newspaper publishing. One deterrent was the English tax on newspapers, which had been doubled from twopence to fourpence: another was his ignorance of the wider scope of the English press world. He must tread gently. Pulling up his Guernsey roots was already venture enough. Before he could think of setting up with the printers from Barnstaple he must feel his way in a safer line, preferably one that was already familiar to him.

# CHAPTER II

## *Prospecting in London*

AFTER Waterloo a deep depression lay over England. European countries were too poor to buy her exports, the National debt was £860 million, and demobilization increased unemployment. Not for the only time in British history, victory failed to pay. The political front was equally discouraging. The monarch was mad, and his dissolute family so disliked that a London crowd mobbed his son, the Prince Regent. In Whitehall the system of representation was chaotically unfair. Reforms were needed everywhere. Feeling against the Government rose into a crescendo culminating in the Peterloo massacres of 1819, when the authorities lost their heads and used military force against unarmed crowds in Manchester.

It was against this bleak background that Thomas de la Rue, now twenty-five, chose to arrive in London with his family to seek his fortune. His entry into the capital was marked only by the legend in the *London Street Directory*:

'De la Rue T. 40 Crown St. Finsbury Square:
Straw hat manufacturer'.

At first sight the veering in direction from Thomas's printing activities in Guernsey to straw hat-making in London is startling, but we can find an explanation.

During the course of 1813 and 1814 Thomas, casting his editorial eye down the weekly list of advertisements to be inserted in the *Miroir Politique*, came across several of a similar nature. In October 1813 he read: 'Wanted immediately an apprentice to a

19

Milliner. Apply at the house now occupied by Mr John Champion opposite the Market place . . .' In February 1814: 'Ann Deschamps and Rachel Robert take the liberty of informing the Ladies and their friends in general that they are on the point of receiving from London a new assortment of *straw* bonnets and that they have taken a shop in the house of Mr Levrier at the top of the market which they intend opening on 25th March next where they will make and mend all sorts of straw bonnets'. On April 5th 1814 Catharine Allez begged to inform her ladies that the fruits of an expedition to London included 'an assortment of Straw, Chip and Leghorn bonnets from the first manufacturers'.

As the *Miroir Politique*'s sole editorial staff consisted of Thomas he unquestionably read these advertisements carefully – if only to count the number of words they contained. What is more, in each case he was connected with the advertiser. John Champion was his brother-in-law, Mr Levrier was also related by marriage, and the Allez's belonged to his mother's family. Thus Thomas was informed on millinery matters long before he left Guernsey. Not only did he know about straw bonnets, but he had also learned at first hand from his relations the favourable prospects of the straw hat trade in London.

\*       \*       \*

Whereas Pepys had considered the straw hat to be rustic, and described an actress at the Duke's theatre as being 'dressed like a country maid with a straw hat on', by the eighteenth century *A Ladies' Dictionary* thought straw hats necessary to the feminine adornment. During the Napoleonic wars the scarcity of other materials accelerated the increase in the straw hat trade. Traditionally bonnets had been made from beaver fur. All over the Continent the hat industry was now, however, bewailing an international shortage of beavers. Europe looked to America. But this source of supply had been interrupted by the war of 1812–14. More attention was therefore focused on the hitherto lowlier straw. *Faute de mieux* the *chapeau de paille* was the answer. Balzac's sister, Laura, found it important enough to mention to her brother. In 1819 she wrote excitedly to Honoré: 'Grandmamma has made us a present of three stitched straw hats, the kind that are being worn now; they're marvellous, you can guess how proud we are . . .' Where France led, England followed. Finding itself *à la mode* the straw hat became subject to the whim of the fashionable *élite*. It was precisely this gamble of being one jump ahead of fashion which appealed to Thomas; because of it he nearly suffered disaster. Commenting a couple of decades later on this stage of his career *Chambers' Journal* pronounced, with a typically Victorian interest in other people's misfortunes, 'In consequence of the successive changes in fashion this ingenious person was several times ruined'.

Thomas did everything he could think of to make his bonnets a success, recording his various efforts in his big Barnstaple notebook. He tried to make them waterproof, and in consequence spent some time examining Mr Macintosh's patent 'for rendering substances impervious to water'. He looked at a substitute for leather invented by a Mr Hancock, and wondered whether silk hats could be made to imitate leghorn ones. He noted the recipe for a special dye concocted by a Monsieur Le Roi of St Germain, and himself brought a breath of refreshing country air into Finsbury when pondering the best methods of obtaining superlative straw:

'At the end of Spring and beginning of Summer when the ears of corn sprout out but are still green, the plants are to be cut off close to the roots, or, which the patentees prefer, to be picked up out of the ground; they are then to be made into small bundles containing each about 150 straws which are to be spread out like fans and exposed to the air and sun on grass land . . .'

In Thomas's jottings the apparently unrelated interests of paper and straw start to overlap around 1825. He contemplates the employment of straw in the manufacture of paper, noting down a French patent for the process. He himself experiments with paper bonnets. These were nothing new. As far back as the 1730s Benjamin Franklin had advertised bonnet papers. Their significance for this history is that Thomas was already pre-occupied with the problems of paper, and with printing – especially colour-printing. He begins by writing up an experiment in the production of chrome yellow, and waxes increasingly lyrical over his different dyes: 'The best white I have produced yet', he cries triumphantly. 'This is really beautiful'. After describing how he treated 'enamelled plain and fancy papers', he lets fall where his ultimate interest lies. In 1828 there appears this item: 'Adding a little talc in the liquor will add more brilliancy – it stands well – it is what I proposed to myself for *playing Cards*'.

Here is the first mention of the commodity which was to turn Thomas's hat venture into a business house of many mansions. He was still officially listed as a 'wholesale dealer in leghorns, chips and straws', but his mind was not really on his millinery. As early as 1824 he had essayed some embossed bookbinding – his name is stamped upon an album produced that year. The Jurors' Report on the 1851 Exhibition states that 'leather covers embossed in elaborate and beautiful patterns by means of fly presses were introduced by M. Thouverin in Paris about 1825 and almost simultaneously in this country by Messrs Remnant and Co. and by Mr de la Rue'.

No patent for this embossing was ever taken out in England. Bookbinding authorities here believe it was the French who led the way in this field. One might therefore deduce that Thomas studied the intricate process in France. It was not the sort of thing which could be learned by correspondence.

Other things point to Thomas's absence across the Channel in the 1820s. There are his notebook entries written in French about the 'teinte noir' from St Germain, and M. Louis Lambert's ideas

22

on straw and paper. His son Warren writes from Paris in 1830, completely settled at school there, and *au fait* with the national scene to an extent which suggests he had been viewing it at close quarters for some time. He assumes that his father's knowledge of French politics is equally up to date: 'Algiers is the only word that we hear in Paris, "Que va-t-on faire d'Algiers?" is the general theme of conversation'. He alludes to a forthcoming parental visit which is clearly by no means Thomas's first. Greetings are sent from his father's Parisian friends, and a request for him to bring one of the ladies a small bottle of aromatic vinegar.

It is unlikely that Thomas would have sent his son and heir blindly to a French school without having looked it over first and weighed its merits against those of other schools. Warren's education at one of the best establishments in France was a major investment for Thomas. It is significant that he chose the College of Ste Barbe, because it laid unusual emphasis on science. He was perceptive enough to see that even at the age of twelve Warren had a highly inventive turn of mind, and he worked out how this could best be put to serve the family business. All his life Thomas liked value for money; instinct warned him against placing his boy in an English public school, where, for de la Rue purposes, the emphasis was still too heavy on the arts. Therefore he considered the added expense of the *va-et-vient* involved in attending a French school justified if the latter were to develop his son's particular scientific talents to their maximum advantage. The parental attitude is reflected in Warren's letter: 'I perceive now that the French education is much superior to the English'.

Since barely a penny had been spent on Thomas's own education, it is not surprising that he should want to see for himself what his child was getting in return for the outlay at the College of Ste Barbe.

Although his relations with his children grew increasingly distant – the tone of Warren's school letter is already merely one of respect and not of affection – nevertheless, where business interests were involved, he would go to endless pains over his family. It is evident that he made fairly frequent personal visits to Paris to oversee the upbringing of his eldest son.

Another fact suggests that Thomas was away a good deal during the first half of the 1820s. There were no new de la Rues. Unless Thomas on the one hand was suffering from an incapacity of which we remain politely unaware, or Jane on the other was afflicted by an unbroken chain of gynaecological problems from 1818 until 1825, the year when William Frederick was born, it might be reasonable to suppose that she and Thomas were not seeing much of each other. Both before and after that period, junior de la Rues arrived at regular intervals.

Throughout the decade of the twenties Jane was kept busy enough changing homes. She moved her household up Crown Street, Finsbury, starting at number 40 and ending up at 65 in 1829. As the street no longer exists it is not possible to tell whether the moves were for better or for worse. A Victorian employee of the firm remembered that the family originally lived over a small hat warehouse 'in a dingy side street'.

Although shops were tending to move westwards, in and around the City it was still customary for a family business to have a warehouse on the ground floor, offices on the first floor, and living quarters on the second floor. Things were crowded on the de la Rue's top floor in Finsbury. In 1828 and 1829 Jane had produced two more children. Although Warren was away at school there were five other brothers and sisters to be fitted in over the warehouse.

When the wind blew in a certain direction, the malt from Whitbread's brewery in Chiswell Street gave off a smell like hot jam. In nearby Bunhill Row the brewery drays were constantly slipping on the cobble stones and getting stuck against the carts of the local carriers coming in the opposite direction, to the accompaniment of a chorus of oaths from their drivers. The pavements were filled with jostling crowds. More and more people, like Thomas himself, were leaving the rural areas for the cities. In the first half of the nineteenth century the population of London was doubling itself. It endured sanitary arrangements whose inadequacy increased as numbers swelled. There was a constant risk of fire. Thomas himself had one in 1840, as a result of which he claimed that £9,000 worth of damage was done to his warehouse, stock and offices. There was never enough water and even something as respectable as the Bank of England only got washed once a month. For Thomas and Jane all this was a far cry from Guernsey and Devon.

Finsbury was good in parts like the curate's egg. The 'dinginess' of Crown Street gave on to fashionable Finsbury Square which caused Tallyho to observe in *Real Life in London*: 'Here at least is a proof that TASTE and ELEGANCE are not entirely excluded from a civic residence . . .' The borough boasted several theatres of which only Sadlers Wells remains. Its inhabitants ranged at different times from Charles Lamb and George Cruickshank to Du Maurier and Livingstone. In his heyday Beau Brummel once attended a ball there, given by a Mrs Thompson.

As his own boss, and a master tradesman, Thomas ought to have been reasonably well off. But with his growing family he was rapidly approaching a time for decision. The top floor over the hat warehouse could not contain them all indefinitely. Should he carry on with straw bonnets or turn to stationery? He compromised and did both.

\*     \*     \*

In 1830 Thomas took a plunge into the stationery business in partnership with a Samuel Cornish and a William Frederick Rock, the men from Barnstaple. They set up in Queen Street, Finsbury, and for the first time Thomas bore the name of card-maker. He and his partners were described as 'Cardmakers, Hot Pressers and

Enamellers'. 'Hot Pressing' was the production of a glossy surface between two plates. The 'enamelling' referred to the hard, smooth finish given to the paper of the playing cards.

We know little of partner Cornish except for a contemporary reference to him as an 'erratic genius'. Mr Rock is less shadowy. The details of his successful business career are gratefully preserved by the North Devon Athenaeum, his crowning bequest to Barnstaple. This houses a museum and a major library, regarding which, as a high-minded bachelor, Mr Rock had firm ideas and a decided objection to the establishment of a ladies' room. 'It would be', he said, 'at the best a mere place of female gossip'.

Mr Rock was a character of some considerable calibre. Thomas was closer to him than to his other partner. He appears to have named his second son, William Frederick, after him, and it was with Rock and not Cornish that he chose to continue in the straw hat business. It is possible that Rock already had some knowledge of the latter trade before he came to London, since the plaiting of straw was a Devon industry.

Both men were as yet unwilling to stake their all upon card-making, and thought it prudent to maintain their straw hat line for another five years. Rock's was probably the more restraining hand of the two, for even at this early stage Thomas was happy to have as many irons in the fire as possible. We have already noticed that he was interested in bookbinding. Remembering the bibliomania which had swept London a few years earlier Thomas, together with a Mr Balne of Gracechurch Street, produced a large royal 8vo edition of the New Testament in 1829 'twenty-five copies of which were in pure gold powder'. The commentary which they chose to accompany it was that of the seventeenth century Nonconformist divine, Matthew Henry, a curiously prophetic choice as far as the firm was concerned – for it was the same Rev. Henry who coined the expression 'Fountain Pen': 'So that without any further Care they received Oil as fast as they wasted it – as in those in which we call Fountain Inkhorns or Fountain Pens'. (Zachariah IV 2).

As a *tour de force* the volume amazed the bibliophiles. Even as late as 1851 it was still agreed that there was nothing to equal it. Unfortunately the public did not feel equal to the price, which was £15 a copy. One, given to William IV and Queen Adelaide at Brighton, is thought to have been presented by Thomas personally as an accession tribute. Timperley's *Dictionary of Printers and Printing* reckoned it to be a 'typographical wonder', the gold alone being worth five guineas, and two years having been employed on its making. Only one copy was actually sold, alas. Lord Spencer bought one for his fine library at Althorp.

Thomas was left with a quantity of gold powder on his hands. The original idea had been to strike off 30,000 copies of the work. Only 104 emerged. In 1834 he tried to issue a second edition with the left-overs, and a third in 1836. The parishioners of Windsor subscribed to buy one which they presented to the Bishop of Colombo, but few ordinary individuals could afford such a luxury. Thomas had been over-optimistic about marketing it. Even so the venture was not entirely unprofitable. For the first time the name of De La Rue became associated with *le grand luxe*. Thomas was launched in 'quality' trade.

\*　　　\*　　　\*

An offshoot of the 'gold' affair was the involvement of 'De La Rue and partners' in legal proceedings. On July 18th 1831, the case was heard at the Court of Exchequer of 'Horner v. De La Rue and others'. Mr Horner claimed that in the course of manufacturing the gold New Testament his stereotype plates were ruined by printing on the hard enamelled vellum found for him by Mr de la Rue. To add insult to injury, the latter had sent him a copy of his own work, so to speak, for which he had the affrontery to charge him 12 guineas. Mr de la Rue had threatened to sue him when he did not settle. Mr Horner's temper could not have been improved by the fact that a copy of the work 'excited the admiration of the Court so much' that all proceedings came to a halt while it was passed through the hands of the Bench, the Bar and the Jury. The wretched plaintiff had to bide his time until 'the curiosity of the Court having been gratified, the proceedings resumed'. The jury conferred briefly together, and a verdict was returned in favour of the defendant. Not for the last time Thomas appeared to have a judge and jury eating out of his hand. At the conclusion of the trial 'the learned Judge expressed a hope that the defendant would be able to furnish him with a copy of the work, the elegance of which he greatly admired'. Whether His Lordship was hinting a trifle greedily that he expected to be given a copy *gratis*, or whether Thomas had found himself an unexpected customer we are never told, nor does it matter. De La Rue could smile complacently at so public an appreciation of their craftsmanship.

\*     \*     \*

At the time that Thomas was entering his first partnership his youngest brother, Paul de la Rue, arrived from Guernsey and settled round the corner in Lamb's Conduit Street. For Jane this was a welcome event as she now had the companionship of her youngest sister Sarah, Paul's wife.

Paul also traded as a manufacturer of leghorns and straws. Thomas evidently thought the straw hat trade still flourishing enough for his brother to embark upon; had he thought otherwise he would have advised him against the move. A close relationship existed between them, Thomas either employing or helping his younger brother throughout the first half of his career.

With the appearance of Paul, Thomas and partner Rock changed their title in the *Street Directory* from 'Straw hat manufacturers' to 'Wholesale dealers in leghorns, chips and straws'. Presumably they supplied Paul with the materials for making the hats. Whatever the arrangement, it was to Paul's satisfaction because he stayed put in the Lamb's Conduit Street business for the next ten years.

*    *    *

In 1831 a momentous event for Thomas took place quietly at Somerset House. As was required for duty purposes he registered an ace of spades there. This was the first public appearance of a De La Rue playing card. Early the following year, all the experimenting and the work recorded in his notebook bore fruit. 'His present most Excellent Majesty King William the Fourth' granted him a Royal Letters Patent for 'certain improvements in making or manufacturing and ornamenting playing cards' in the second year of his reign.

Up until this time playing cards had either been stencilled by hand in water colours or printed in one colour and then hand tinted. Either way the process was inevitably expensive, laborious and inaccurate. To colour fifty-two cards by hand with identical precision was beyond human possibility.

The first of a long line of De La Rue patents, Thomas's playing-card 'Improvements' are twelve pages long. At first sight they are verbose and cloudy. On pages nine and ten of the specification Thomas gives a detailed account of the preparation of coloured printing inks. He then affirms that as other oils will do for these colours 'it will not be requisite' to do what he has in fact just done, i.e. give a detailed account of the preparation of coloured printing inks.

This verbosity is offset by a charming tendency to describe à la Mrs Beeton:

'Take one gallon of old linseed oil (the older the better) and boil it very slowly for three or four hours in an iron pot or vessel, occasionally igniting it and stirring during the whole process with an iron ladle. In some instances I find it necessary to dip a few slices of stale bread just prior to ebulation taking place which facilitates the operation . . .'

Determined to ignore a prime Voltairian rule ('If you want to bore the reader tell him everything'), Thomas instructs us how to boil our pot.

'The manner of igniting is as follows:
When it is found that by applying a light to a surface it will take fire the pot or vessel is removed from the fire . . . when it goes out the pot is again placed on the fire – should the ignition be two (*sic*) violent, it must and may be stopped by placing a cover over the top of the pot containing the oil. When cold it should be the consistency of very thick treacle'.

The real contributions of Thomas's 'Improvements' were the 'Ring',[1] the superior quick drying oil-inks employed, the new method of glazing the cards by passing them between copper sheets through powerful rollers instead of the antique method of glazing by friction with a flint, and the use of enamelled paper.

However amateur the presentation of Thomas's patent may have been, it remains a landmark inside the firm's history, and, indeed, outside. As a result of it Thomas became known not only as 'the father of the English playing card' but was claimed by some to be largely responsible for modern English colour printing. Word of his achievement was to spread to the Continent: 'De La Rue, Cartier à Londres, a deposé un brevet pour un procédé permettant de colorier les cartes avec les couleurs à l'huile . . . en France ce procédé ne sera couramment employé qu'après 1850 environ . . .' conceded a French playing card expert.

In his turn Mr de la Rue would have conceded that his forte was innovation rather than invention. It is not easy to point the dis-

[1] One of the problems of colour printing was that of 'register', i.e. ensuring that the pink of a royal face on a court card neither overlapped its outline nor failed to meet it, thereby engendering an ugly white gap. Thomas solved this by making a steel block or 'ring' into which was cut an oblong the exact size of a playing card. When a measured piece of lead was inserted in this aperture and pressed down on to the original plate the lead, now bearing the image, could be extracted and fifty-two reproductions in reverse fitted together in four plates of precise size.

tinction between the two; every invention must owe something to existing ones. Thomas's genius lay in his ability to adapt other people's ideas to the immediate benefit of his own merchandise. For instance no sooner had John George Christ invented enamelled paper in 1829 than Thomas perceived where he could put it to good use, and pounced on it for his playing cards.

An early experimenter in colour printing was William Savage who published *Hints on Decorative Printing* in two parts in 1816 and 1823. By June 1832 Thomas really knew his subject and felt sufficiently confident to tear these 'Hints' to shreds. In his notebook that month he writes a series of scathing observations on 'Mr Savage's recipe':

'I rubbed a piece of blank paper on the pages of his work, and as I anticipated the colour came off as freely as if it had been printed an hour!' tho it had been printed for ten years! . . . I copy his table of colours more as a subject of inquiry than to follow, for as he has erred so much in having recourse to a substance the properties of which he was evidently ignorant he must be distrusted by all practical men'.

In the course of correcting Mr Savage's mistakes Thomas added his own improvements to the process of colour printing; it was these which provided a basis for his first De La Rue patent.

If Thomas, bubbling over with self-confidence, makes us wary of over-estimating him, we must also be careful to give him his due. Burch writing in 1910 declared: 'It must not be forgotten that in 1835 there was, except Baxter (then comparatively unknown) no colour printer in London save De La Rue'.

Strangely enough, George Baxter, who came from a Sussex family of printers and antiquarian booksellers established in Lewes, also lived in Finsbury. He registered a patent 'For Improvements in Producing Coloured Steel Plate, Copper Plate and other Impressions'. Baxter's and Thomas's patents overlap to a remarkable degree. Thomas's preceded Baxter's by four years. In this instance Thomas was unquestionably the forerunner. But in the field of colour printing he chose to restrict himself to playing cards, whereas Baxter's speciality was the production of coloured prints for books.

Reassured that his neighbour was not a commercial enemy Thomas had nothing to fear in comparing notes with Baxter. It would have been another story had they been competing against each other. The Baxter family would have made efficient adversaries. In 1831, Gideon Mantell, a Sussex surgeon, wrote in his journal: 'Up all night; amused myself by scribbling some "Plain Rules for the Cholera" finished them at breakfast and Baxter printed them before night, pretty expeditious'. Fortunately for the firm of De La Rue, the Baxters did not carry their expeditiousness into Thomas's camp, and he was free to mount his solitary assault on the public taste in playing cards.

Never one to suffer fools gladly, Thomas was not easy to work for during this period. In 1832, the year the patent came out, he records: 'William Campack was detected on the 8th Nov on a Thursday'. In following a recipe for 'Card Preparation' the unfortunate man had misjudged the amount of gum arabic, and as a result the paper had turned out soft. Mr Campack was given notice of dismissal on the spot and by Saturday, only two days later, had been removed altogether. Months of hard work on the playing card patent had not improved Thomas's nerves.

\*     \*     \*

Thomas was not content to rest for one minute on his 'Improvements to Playing Cards'. He liked to keep things on the move; *perpetuum mobile* was his watchword. In the years between 1832 and 1835 he set about altering the actual designs of playing card faces, which had remained unchanged for generations.

Where angels would have feared Mr de la Rue now dared to tread, trying cunningly to change the habits of the card player, that most conservative of mortals. His alterations were not

1. Fountain Street, St Peter Port, Guernsey, from a sketch made in 1799. According to an 1820 street plan Eleazar de la Rue's house is on the left

2. Special 'golden' edition of the *Sun* newspaper printed by De La Rue to celebrate Queen Victoria's Coronation, 1838

Head of Queen Victoria De La Rue receipt stamp, 1853

drastic. He simply tried to put a little life into his kings, queens and knaves. By tradition these had always had blank, wooden faces; Thomas attempted to get some sort of expression into the royal eyes. He modernised the court-dress slightly, and gave his queens feet.

In the market De La Rue wanted to capture, whist was the bingo of the day. *Mrs Battle's Opinions on Whist* by Charles Lamb presents the kernel of the nut Thomas was trying to crack. For Mrs Battle whist was 'her business, her duty, the thing she came into the world to do – and she did it. She unbent her mind afterwards – over a book'. Whist-mania spread, casting a spell over people with whose 'illusion we are as mightily concerned as those whose stake is crowns and kingdoms'. Up and down the country all that the whist players asked for was a 'clean fire, a clean hearth and the rigour of the game'. In their choice of playing card weapons they were reactionary; they wanted to get on with the fight and not be diverted.

'Why two colours even', cries Mrs Battle, 'when the mark of the suit would distinguish without it?'

Charles Lamb goes to Thomas's defence: 'But the eye, my dear madam', he replies, 'is agreeably refreshed with variety. Man is not a creature of pure reason – he must have his senses delightfully appealed to'. He examines the colours and antics of the court cards and pronounces firmly:

'All these might be dispensed with and with their naked names upon the drab paste board the game might go on very well, pictureless, but the *beauty* of cards would be extinguished for ever'.

Mrs Battle was an extreme case, but she pointed to Thomas the way he should go. At considerable cost he bowed to her. He is said to have 'incurred heavy losses in the endeavour to create a more elegant taste in playing cards', losses which contributed to the financial debacle in which he was shortly to find himself.

Ostensibly he allowed the Mrs Battles to have their way. The faces of his new playing cards obediently reverted to the desired conventions. Once more they became expressionless, and the queens lost their feet again. Thomas appeared to have capitulated. So intent were the players on their game, however, that before they had realised it, Mr de la Rue had wrought some changes in their paste boards after all. Quick to take the point that there was no future in altering the fronts of the cards, he changed his tack. He revolutionised the backs instead. In so doing he proved that he could do a smart about-turn; at one moment he was facing an expensive mistake, at the next a trade success, a manoeuvre that he performed so smoothly that the public was hardly conscious that he had suffered a fall in the process.

\*       \*       \*

Thomas de la Rue had natural good taste; he had neither the education nor the money to acquire it otherwise. He showed himself to be aware of the coming trend in design away from eighteenth century classical simplicity towards the beginnings of Victorian elaboration. Yet somehow he managed to prevent his products from suffering an overdose of decoration, and maintained in them 'a refined character' which, thought a visiting journalist, 'is a striking proof that a better, a purer order of things is arising among us'. He was something of a connoisseur. One of his loves was Wedgwood china, which he started to collect when he came to London.

He was on the look-out for original ideas for playing card backs 'choosing some of the best artists in London and giving them as much as twenty or thirty pounds for a design no larger than a hand's breadth'. According to a visiting journalist 'Mr de la Rue's idea had been to excite and cultivate the public taste'. In these 'more elegant forms of printing', noted the impressed writer, 'formerly in England few or no manufacturers thought of going to the expense of employing designers'. They had merely copied from French originals.

Thomas was *avant-garde* in employing his own artists; he even managed to improve their status, which according to *Chambers' Edinburgh Journal* could hardly have been lower:

'In the chief manufacturing towns there may have been here and there a dissipated man of genius who, when he could be laid hold of quite sober, would for a guinea or so, furnish a design, such as it was . . .'

His preoccupation with designs for playing card backs was not entirely aesthetic. Until he arrived on the scene the backs, being plain, revealed flaws all too easily. This was a source of constant annoyance to the players. A recognizable bump on a knave of diamonds, for instance, could spoil the sport for a beady-eyed Mrs Battle. Thomas's all-over patterns camouflaged any such potential give-aways. Not that there were many flaws in his cards; the new smooth-surfaced enamelled paper ensured there were no 'hills and valleys'.

*     *     *

Until 1833 the partnership of De La Rue, Cornish and Rock had been installed in Crown Street. In September of that year the partners rented 110 Bunhill Row, Finsbury, from James Esdaile for £230 per annum, and De La Rue became associated with the street which was to remain its business home for the next century. Thomas's new landlord was yet another link with the West Country. Esdaile's Bank handled West Country agencies including one for Barnstaple.

Thomas did not take up the rental of Bunhill Row until 1834, probably because he was not only changing house, but also partners. For twelve, crowded, transitional months he had all his interests under one roof at 20 Finsbury Place. It not only housed the de la Rue family, and the old partnership of 'De La Rue and Rock' in its final appearance as 'Leghorn Manufacturers', but also Thomas's new partnership of 'De La Rue, James and Rudd', listed as 'Cardmakers, Embossers and Wholesale Fancy Stationers'.

The embossing referred to 'paper hangings' for which Thomas was working on a new process.

By 1835 Messrs Cornish and Rock had bowed amicably out, Mr Rock, we know, having made £5,000 through his three year association with Thomas. At the same time that her husband and his new partners were establishing themselves in 110 Bunhill Row, Jane moved next door into No 108. Here at last she had a house to herself. There was no warehouse underneath, no coming and going of customers and errand boys up the stairs. She could enjoy the luxury of unleashing her family from the attics and allowing them the freedom of four whole storeys. Bunhill Row was an agreeable street with a distinguished history of its own. The shaded expanse of Bunhill Fields opposite, with its avenues of plane trees, dated its burial ground from the time of a prehistoric tumulus, hence the name Bone Hill. In the seventeenth century it was opened to provide a cemetery for London dissenters and contains the graves of Bunyan and Defoe. Down the road the Honourable Artillery Company set up its headquarters, its drill ground providing another open space. In the same street the blind Milton composed *Paradise Regained,* and it was here that he died soon afterwards.

This was the site that Thomas chose for the founding of his house and dynasty. Here he and his sons, grandsons and great-grandsons mapped the fortunes of De La Rue, until nearly all Bunhill Row and considerable portions of neighbouring property became assimilated into their little empire.

# CHAPTER III

# Foundation difficulties

In 1835 Thomas de la Rue seemed secure. He had moved into fine premises, greatly improved the lot of his family, and taken the decision to put straw bonnets behind him for ever. Now he could concentrate where his talents and interests lay. He had satisfactorily terminated one partnership, and was well enough pleased with one of his new partners, Isaac James, to accept him as a future son-in-law. The other, James Rudd, judging by his name, (a common one in and around Bishop's Nympton) was probably yet another of his numerous West Country connections.

The move, however, from one sphere of business to another proved far from easy. Thomas had now been nursing the young stationery business for seven years, maintaining his straw bonnet trade in case of adversity. In 1830, while he was solely engaged in millinery, things had been prosperous enough. Warren wrote from Paris to request his father that his younger brother William Frederick, then aged five, join him at the college of Sainte Barbe as soon as he was old enough; also that his sister Jane be allowed to 'take a little trip to France'. Invariably considerate, even Warren did not feel he was asking for an extravagance. He added confidently: 'I am sure you will have no objection . . .'

Later on in the 1830s the picture began to change radically and there was no question of such indulgences. In 1837 William Frederick found himself put to work in Bunhill Row at the age of twelve, receiving a pound's worth of 'wages to 29th April'. In June his sister Jane, far from enjoying any French junketings, was paid £6 6s 5d 'for cutting bands' for playing cards. In August even Jane senior emerged from the family house in No 108, and rendered unspecified services in No 110, for which she received £7 10s. If Thomas was forced to put all available family hands to the pump something was seriously wrong with the affairs of De La Rue, James and Rudd.

1837 was not only a bad year for a young business trying to gather impetus. It happened to be a difficult one all round. Thomas was not alone in feeling a financial draught. The investors of England were due for a series of shocks. There was near panic in America, where three hundred banks failed within the year. A trade fluctuation of no ordinary dimensions was building up thunder clouds.

One of the English banks to fail in this year was Esdailes. Esdaile's records for this period have not survived; but knowing Thomas's liking for the personal connection, the bank of his choice would have been that of his landlord and neighbour James Esdaile; indeed, the latter being agent for Barnstaple banks, Thomas was almost certainly recommended to him before he ever arrived in London. This being the case, De La Rue, James and Rudd would have lost any deposits they had lodged at the bank.

\*　　　\*　　　\*

The first sign that there was anything amiss in Bunhill Row came in April 1837. On the 29th an entry in the account books under the heading *De La Rue, James and Rudd Estate* notes that: 'De La Rue and Company assigned all machinery and stock in trade, book debts to T. B. Crompton and William Sedgewick'. The names of these two gentlemen were about to be linked with Thomas's continuously for the next two years. They were to be his two chief creditors. It is interesting that in spite of the prolonged haggling that ensued both characters remained friends of Thomas's, Mr Crompton actually expiring in Thomas's country house some twenty years later. After reading the solicitors' reports of the two-year legal battle, with Messrs Crompton and Sedgewick in one camp, and Thomas in the other, one is astonished that the opposing parties ever remained on speaking terms.

Mr Crompton and Mr Sedgewick were not small time merchants dunning Thomas for petty bills, nor were they the sort of men who would easily succumb to his charm. They were worthy opponents. Thomas Bonsor Crompton, the principal creditor, was a millionaire cotton manufacturer and paper miller whose family had lifted the Lancashire hamlets of Farnworth and Prestolee out of rural obscurity into urban prosperity. He was a considerable figure, not only in the provinces but in London, where as an off-shoot from his paper business he found himself 'at one time or another proprietor of most of the established London newspapers including the *Morning Post*'. He was said to 'despise indulgence but to respect industry and persevering effort whenever he found them'. There was no doubt that he respected Mr de la Rue very much indeed.

The first round of the legal contest of Crompton and Sedgewick versus De La Rue had opened in March 1837. On the 14th of that month Mr William Sedgewick went off to consult his solicitors 'respecting the affairs of Thomas De La Rue and Company as to the expendiency of making a further advance'. Technically the house was called 'De La Rue, James and Rudd', but it will be noticed that Thomas dominated all his partnerships to such an extent that the names of his partners are sometimes overlooked altogether. The use of the word 'further' advance indicates that Mr Sedgewick had made more than one. Thomas's affairs had been in a shaky state long enough to cause alarm. The final crash appears to have been due to the bankruptcy of one of Thomas's customers, a Mr Drew.

In connection with De La Rue affairs Mr Sedgewick is now attended upon almost daily by his solicitors. He tells Mr Crompton of his findings, and the scene of the struggle changes to Bunhill

Row, where, together with their legal advisers, they spend hours locked in combat with an unyielding Thomas. His prospective son-in-law Isaac James, emerges, not unnaturally, as his loyal supporter, but his other partner seems to have been conducting clandestine meetings on the side. There is an entry in the solicitors' accounts referring to a somewhat unorthodox attendance upon a solitary 'Mr Rudd at the Castle and Falcon, 6s 8d for conferring and 5s 6d cab hire'. If it cost 5s 6d to get there, James Rudd had gone out of his way to pick a rendezvous which was not in the environs of Bunhill Row.

By the end of April matters are coming to a head. The indications are that Thomas is anxious to be shot of outside partners and is impatient to set up on his own again. He has taken to his bosom a distinguished employee called Alfred Augustus Fry, a man of impressive scholarship, the creator, together with his son Danby, of a 'new arrangement and classification of all the words in Johnson's *English Dictionary*'. Alfred Augustus was the firm's accountant. When Thomas did not feel like attending the creditors' meetings he sent Alfred Augustus instead and later rewarded him with a directorship.

Perhaps it should be added that since his salary was £125 in arrears Mr Fry was not a totally disinterested party. Money was also owing to Jane's young nephew, William Warren (£16) and to the senior traveller Jonah Nathan (£92 6s). Paid or not, they all stuck by Thomas for the rest of their careers. Thomas may have been difficult but he commanded respectful loyalty.

On the 2nd May a notice appeared in the *Gazette* of the dissolution of the partnership of De La Rue, James and Rudd. To show there were no hard feelings Thomas threw a celebration in honour of his ex-partners, which according to the account books went on for several days at a cost of £7 14s, more than a week of his subsequent salary. Not normally renowned for his freehandedness he allowed joy on this occasion to be unconfined. The flinging of economy to the winds at a time of extremely straitened circumstances signifies the extent of his relief at being free.

\*    \*    \*

His second partnership dissolved, Thomas de la Rue, with his lieutenants Fry and Nathan, set about trying to put his house in order. Messrs Crompton and Sedgewick were impressed by their joint efforts. On 6th May 1837, they wrote to Jonah Nathan authorising him to collect all book debts owing to the firm by previous customers and advising him at the same time to ask all such clients to maintain their dealings with De La Rue. 'The business now placed upon a firm footing', they urged, 'you can have no difficulty in showing to your friends the advantage of confirming their connection with the house'.

The future looked deceptively brighter. Even the hardheaded creditors were optimistic. But the fortunes of De La Rue were fated to sink still lower. On May 26th Thomas was actually arrested for debt. This being before the days of public companies, he was personally responsible for the firm's liabilities, and answerable to them with such worldly goods as he possessed. There is no clue as to the person at whose insistence the arrest was made. His private and his commercial affairs were intertwined, and it might have been a purely domestic bill, such as his grocer's, which toppled him.

Whoever it was that was dunning him, Thomas was lodged in a Bailiff's House. Such a house was also called a 'Lock-up' or 'Sponging House'. Kept by a Bailiff, with the assistance of his Bum, it occupied a position halfway between freedom and actual imprisonment in the Fleet. Some people considered a period of residence in a place of this nature to be salutary. Mr Maxwell declared: 'it invigorates genius, concentrates ingenuity and stimulates invention'. By the impatience of his nature unsuited to the enjoyment of such circumstances, it was fortunate for Thomas that he was only left to cool his heels for one night in the Lock-up before Mr Sedgewick, with his indefatigable solicitor in tow, came galloping to the rescue in a hansom cab. 'After much trouble', notes the latter, 'we obtained the liberation of Mr de la Rue giving undertaking to officer etc'.

Mr Sedgewick proceeded to pay the fine of one guinea, which Mr de la Rue did not appear to have on him, and was reimbursed by the faithful Alfred Augustus Fry. The fact that only the fine was paid, and not the debt, suggests that a substantial amount was owed.

Mr Sedgewick sprang swiftly to Thomas's aid because his bankruptcy was the last thing that he and Mr Crompton desired. All they wanted was repayment of what he owed them, which in Crompton's case amounted to over £9,500. Had they persisted in having Thomas declared bankrupt, several years must have elapsed before he could hope to obtain his discharge, and they would thereby virtually have killed the goose which, they were convinced, was a potential layer of golden eggs. The sooner Mr de la Rue was assisted back into his nesting box in Bunhill Row, the quicker they would get their money back.

At this juncture Thomas was scarcely in a position to bargain but this was what he attempted to do. Back and forth swayed the negotiations through June, July, August and September, paused, and then opened up again the following year in June 1838. Although he was arguing from an inferior position Thomas flatly affirmed that he was not going to accept the creditors' terms. The deadlock concerned the assignment of the rights in Thomas's white lead patent; for weeks he fought for them tooth and nail.

The white lead patent was of much importance to Thomas. Ever since 1833 he had been working on John Duisbury's method of producing white lead. It was a vital ingredient used in the enamelling of the new playing cards, but at a guinea an ounce it was inordinately expensive. Thomas experimented with different ways of making the process cheaper. He successfully evolved a process which he patented in 1837, when his financial position was at its worst. He now argued that he was only answerable to his debts with such goods as he possessed at the time of their incurrence, and that anything he earned after that time, such as money received as a result of this latest patent, could not be grabbed by the creditors in lieu of compensation.

The De La Rue recipe for white lead effected an astonishing reduction in price from one guinea to sixpence an ounce. Its fame spread to the Channel Islands, where Thomas's distant career was being followed with interest. A year late with the news the *Guernsey Star* announced on June 11th 1838:

'We are happy to state that Mr de la Rue formerly a printer in this island, and well known as an inventor of the new playing cards, has recently discovered a new method of preparing white lead, the new patent of which he has sold for thirty thousand pounds, reserving to himself one sixteenth of the profits. Many of our readers who know the ingenuity of Mr de la Rue will rejoice that this brilliant success has crowned his labours'.

On this occasion good news travelled faster than bad. No mention was made of current De La Rue disasters. Even if it had heard them mentioned, the *Guernsey Star* preserved a discreet silence concerning the misfortunes of a quick-tempered fellow printer and ex-editor, whom it knew to be notoriously swift to pick a quarrel. Biting his nails while trying to find a way of pacifying his creditors, Thomas must have smiled wanly at the rosy, home-town picture of his current affairs.

Maybe he was invigorated by reading the account. At any rate he came up with fresh suggestions. He concurred in the main with Crompton's and Sedgewick's proposals, notably the basic one that the property of the firm including the complete stock of warehouse and factory be vested in them as trustees for him and his interests. In return Thomas asked Crompton and Sedgewick to guarantee his bills of exchange to tide him over his immediate difficulties, pay him a salary of £6 a week, and allow him to stay on in his house in Bunhill Row.

Temporarily all was sweetness and light with the exception of the monotonous tug-of-war over the white lead. Throughout the legal ping-pong of 1837 and 1838 Thomas managed to apply himself to developing the aforesaid white lead patent, regardless of the current dispute about its ownership. He became bored with the finer points of law involved. Fed up, anxious to be free of the lot, partners and creditors alike, he wanted to be left alone to get on with his work. He had a bruised and battered business to re-establish. To hasten this end he took £150 from the Trust.

Whether he was entitled to this money is debatable. What is certain is that whereas he had no deliberate intention to defraud his creditors, he was plainly unwilling for the scant remains of his house to burn while lawyers fiddled.

By June 10th 1838, his temper was in shreds and his patience exhaused. Crompton's solicitor, James Taylor, recorded testily: 'It came out last night – high words – Mr de la Rue said he would have this day the first opinion in London . . .' This threat was a last ditch stand on Thomas's part, yet his powers of resistance still proved effective. Later in the month even the mighty millionaire Crompton flinched from a direct confrontation with Mr de la Rue and left town in order to avoid the experience. He prevailed upon his co-trustee Sedgewick to do the job for him, and through him offered Mr de la Rue £9,500 for his share of the white lead patent. Thomas bit the hand that was trying to feed him and vehemently refused this, albeit with some reason, since the De La Rue share was worth at least £12,000.

By June 1838 the full amount required to clear the firm's estate was £19,000. Grudgingly admitting that beggars cannot be choosers, Thomas decided to let Crompton have his white lead share for the bargain price of £9,500 after all. At the same time one of the erstwhile debtors to the firm of De La Rue, a Mr Cave, managed to produce the sum of £2,500. At long last things were beginning to look up.

To complete the brightening picture a Mr Charles Button appeared on the scene, and declared himself willing to advance the remaining £7,000 which Thomas needed, plus £1,500 to re-launch him, since: 'he thought it of so much consequence to Mr de la Rue to be free from the Trust'.

There was further discussion about leases in Bunhill Row, but to cut a long story short Crompton and Sedgewick could not but agree to wind up the trust now that all the money was accounted for – at least nearly all. Technically Thomas still owed £2,500 to Crompton, but the latter was only too eager to be quit of his responsibility for the affairs of De La Rue, and he was prepared to accept Thomas's unsecured covenant for this amount. In this, at least, Thomas may be said to have won a victory.

\*       \*       \*

According to *A New System of Practical Domestic Economy founded on Modern Discoveries and from the Private Communications of Persons of Experience*, the weekly salary of £6 allotted to Thomas by Crompton and Sedgewick just about allowed him to live like a 'gentleman'. A single man could do so on £150 a year. A married man with three children needed £250 for his wife to live like a 'lady' and employ one maidservant at £16 a year. With six children Thomas and Jane were borderline cases. To be 'carriage folk' an income of not less than £400 per annum was essential; Thomas was quite equal to this two years later when he was drawing a more comfortable £12 a week. Less than twenty years later he and his family, had they wanted, could have owned carriages galore.

\*       \*       \*

I have purposely lingered over the years 1837 and 1838. Throughout that period it was touch and go whether De La Rue sank or swam. If it had sunk, it is difficult to see how even Thomas, resourceful though he was, could have made yet another start. The fact that the firm swam was his own triumph. To keep the head of a young firm above water, when bigger and older establishments were going under on all sides, was no mean achievement.

The detailed accounts of the solicitors reveal something of his mercurial self, his opportunism, his hot-bloodedness and tenacity. The question of his honesty was never really in doubt, otherwise it is impossible to understand how a shrewd Lancashire tycoon like Crompton could have allowed him the loan of £2,500 purely on his own good word. Thomas did not deliberately set out to sail as close as possible to the wind; but he liked to make sure that no puff was wasted.

So it came about that Mr de la Rue became a free businessman again, and as such lived happily ever after. In spite of all that has been said about his abilities, we are left with a suspicion that however impenetrable his tangled affairs and however black the economic situation of England, somehow, somewhere, Thomas would have landed on his feet. Not least among his attributes he had abundance of the one Napoleon demanded of his generals, the attribute of any successful businessman – luck.

\*　　　\*　　　\*

Surrounded by economic gloom the people of England were hopeful of finding a ray of light in the accession in 1837 of young Victoria to the throne. After the degenerate reigns of her uncles she was, by contrast, associated in their minds with an image of innocent goodness presiding over the dawning of a comparatively golden age; that was how they wished to see her. Pausing from the depressing reading of his balance sheets, Thomas contributed the idea of a golden newspaper to celebrate her Coronation.

On 28th June 1838 the unprecedented phenomenon of the *Sun* newspaper 'printed in gold' was placed before the British public by Thomas de la Rue. Unlike the ill-fated New Testaments it was a sell out. There was such a scramble for commemorative copies that they were being sold at five shillings or more, some even at a guinea.

Thomas had talked Messrs Clowes and Sons of Stamford Street into placing at his disposal 'the printing machines of their Extensive Establishment' – something which, as yet, he lacked in quantity. One hundred thousand *Suns* were printed in Stamford Street and rushed round to De La Rue to be gilded.

In the open yard at Bunhill Row a big marquee was set up to house the operation which lasted six days. Copies were spread over every available space to dry. Fortunately unseasonable wind and rain gave way to hot sun. For the whole rush job over a hundred men and women were employed. Mr Drake, J. Blogg, J. Christ (the enameller) and Mr de la Rue himself between them collected £73 17s overtime. The account books recorded that to print the *Sun* in 'gold', 33 lbs Yellow ink, 10 lbs Varnish, 3 quarts Turpentine, 1 lb 12 ozs Bronze, 6 tons Coals 25s were consumed.

For De La Rue the *Sun* editions were a happy omen. Everything was at last tidied up. In another of his rare bursts of generosity Thomas insisted on making a present to his ex-creditor, William Sedgewick. He gave him six 'golden' *Suns*.

# CHAPTER IV

## *A solid base*

IT was mainly due to Mr Charles Button's loan of £8,500 that the firm was saved. Without this sum De La Rue would have suffered a much longer chapter of accidents, so that for Thomas, Mr Button's advent was more than lucky, it was almost magical. Who was this *deus ex machina* who appeared from nowhere to provide the cash?

Mr Button was a wealthy chemist and importer of 'operative and manufacturing chemical apparatus'. Amongst a variety of interests he listed 'under water cables', sharing a patent for 'Certain Improvements in the Means of Appliances used in the Conveying of Telegraphic Intelligence between Different Places'. One of his scientific papers was entitled 'A Series of Tables of the Elementary and Compound Bodies Systematically Arranged'. His co-author was a young scientist called Warren de la Rue.

So it was not only luck that Thomas had to thank for the change in his fortunes, but something more tangible – his own son. The dramatic supporting move of Mr Button was the first of many occasions when father and firm were to owe a large debt to Warren de la Rue.

Mr Button and young Warren spent a good deal of time together. During the course of their joint studies Charles Button, by many years the senior of the two, became convinced that the firm's expectations were bound to be increased by Warren's inventive gifts. Of these he had seen ample evidence, and on their account alone he felt that De La Rue was worth rescuing.

3. Warren de la Rue by William Troutschold, 1851

4. William Frederick (Colonel Billy) de la Rue by William Troutschold, 1851

When Warren had arrived in France from Finsbury at the age of fourteen he was not, unlike his father, bilingual. He had been born in Guernsey when public affairs in the Court House, as well as church services, were still mainly conducted in French; but at the time of his parents' departure for England he was only two. His Ste Barbe school reports tell us that during his first year in Paris, in 1829, he wrestled manfully with his French, and also did well at arithmetic. His success in these two subjects led his tutors to say, in the language of schoolmasters the world over, that at other things 'il pourra bien faire'. On the whole they considered him a willing student with a natural aptitude for learning. His general reports glowed:

'Cet enfant montre déjà plus de maturité que son age n'en comporte, la conduite tres régulière, caractère bon, sensible, honnête avec ses maîtres et prévenant envers ses petits camarades'. His health was excellent.

A good mixer, upright, dependable, poised and wise beyond his years, little Warren is too good to be true. It is a relief to learn that in his second year he is human enough to relax his efforts and rest on the preceding year's laurels. His French is not progressing so well and his masters detect in him 'certaines légèretés' which force them to administer 'quelques petits reproches'.

Nevertheless, they continue, his bouts of light-heartedness will not seriously affect his work if he can maintain in his private studies the exemplary behaviour he displays in class. They note approvingly that he is 'rempli d'intelligence', and end the Spring Term reports on a prophetic note: 'Cet élève est capable de faire un sujet distingué, qu'il ne manque pas sa destinée'.

In the summer term he is gay at play and serious at work. Although he is slow at drawing and his history is consistently 'faible', the results of his arithmetic examinations are outstanding. By the end of his second year the 'petits reproches' have had the desired effect, and from all sides there is nothing but praise. He now has a positive 'amour de l'étude'. Hereafter his masters cannot complain of his slightest negligence.

Although loaded with panegyrics this paragon of virtue managed to sustain his high spirits. If he occasionally let off steam, by this time he had so captivated his superiors that they dismissed any lapses as being 'ni longs, ni dangereux'. His *joie de vivre* is impressive when placed against the backcloth of the current regime. While living conditions were bad in England, they were tougher still across the Channel. France had not yet recovered from the consequences of Napoleon's ultimate defeat. Life at Ste Barbe was even more spartan than at an equivalent English public school. In weathers of all seasons pupils had nowhere to wash except in the open court yards. When the pipes were frozen, fuel buckets were taken down and filled from the Seine. Yet Warren's kindly nature managed to remain unhardened by these rigours. That he was especially loved by his fellow pupils, as his teachers said, was no small achievement under a highly competitive system which encouraged boys to criticise each other's work.

If the long list of his subsequent honours recorded in the *Dictionary of National Biography* reads like the worthy life of yet another eminent Victorian, his school reports reveal promise of a more unusual personality – one in which warm good humour, gaiety, personal courage and a gift for inspiring affection in all sorts of humans, mingle with the more conventional virtues of his day.

Warren's entry into his father's company was hastened by the 1830 Revolution in France. Middle class moderates decided to push out the reactionary Charles X and install Louis Philippe in his stead. One morning in July the head master of Ste Barbe interrupted the pupils at their lessons to announce the uprising. The Hotel de Ville was already under attack, the day boys were sent home, and some of the seniors joined in the ensuing two days of street fighting. Although he was willing for his son to endure the trials of a foreign college, Thomas evidently thought that to ask him to undergo a revolution as well was too much. After that eventful July there is no further mention of Warren in the school annals. From the point of view of the parental pocket the removal of Charles X occurred at an opportune moment. It provided Thomas, struggling to preserve some sort of equilibrium in his early partnerships, with a decent excuse for bringing his boy home to Finsbury, where his keep would be appreciably cheaper.

*　　*　　*

Warren de la Rue was then in his sixteenth year. The earliest record of his presence in 110 Bunhill Row was his signature in 1835 on the contract of a Thomas Rockett (who was to work 'as a card-maker' for the not inconsiderable sum of 45s per week); so Warren's career in the firm appears to have started around his eighteenth birthday.

Straight away Thomas ensured that his son devoted his spare time to those branches of scientific experiment most likely to develop De La Rue's interest. Warren's first scientific paper dealing with the 'Daniell' electric battery was published when he was twenty-one. It helped lead to the application of electro-plating in typography, which in turn revolutionised security printing.

Warren himself did not benefit materially from this early success, nor were his initial years in the firm guaranteed to raise his financial hopes. By May day, 1837, his salary was already in arrears. He failed to receive his quarterly payment of £26 16s 11d. But in 1839, when he was twenty-three, his patience was reward-ed. He was made a partner, together with his friend, the saviour of De La Rue, Mr Charles Button. Thomas, solvent once more, found £2,965 to stand as Warren's share of the capital. His own share was £6,877 and Mr Button's, the largest, £7,351.

Now that his status as a partner was assured and his salary paid up to date, Warren asked for the hand of nineteen year old Georgiana Bowles. Miss Bowles likewise had been born in Guernsey. Her father, described as 'a gentleman of independent means', had properties in St Peter Port. His fortune had steadily increased when those of grandfather Eleazar de la Rue had conversely been in decline. Like Thomas Mr Bowles moved all his family to London, but backed by considerably larger material assets than the de la Rues possessed. He bought a villa in Islington from which Warren and Georgiana were married at the beginning of 1840.

Young Mrs Warren de la Rue's good looks were of the delicate, Dresden China variety, and upon first meeting her some of her husband's friends were apprehensive about his choice of so fragile though so charming a partner. They did not think that she would be keeping him company for long in this world.

As it turned out, however, it was his beloved Georgie who nursed Warren devotedly through the illnesses of old age, attacking his international correspondence with gusto, and punctiliously answering on his behalf the kind inquiries of scientists from half Europe. A childhood attack of smallpox appeared neither to have weakened her constitution, nor marred her beauty. Travelling tirelessly with Warren, she rattled across Russia in a coach and comforted him in wearisomely drawn out Italian business negotiations, the ultimate success of which, as her brother-in-law justly pointed out, owed more than a little to her patience and tact. Georgiana was a forerunner of a long line of company wives supporting their husbands around the globe. In her nineties she would cut short her enthralling traveller's tales to her grandchildren in order to ask anxiously after Bleriot's progress across the Channel. She died when she was ninety-eight.

\*     \*     \*

de la Rue *fils* was now well launched, on account of his partnership, his happy marriage to Georgiana, and his scientific successes, but de la Rue *père* had no intention of taking a back seat. In 1840 Thomas produced his most visionary contribution yet. Tucked away in his patent for the 'Improvements in printing calicoes and surfaces' are the far-reaching words:

'In printing bankers checks, bills, etc. *bank notes, post office envelopes* or any work requiring great difficulty of invention the wire fabric or tissue may be made with a plain or ornamental ground'. (My italics).

Here was the realisation of the theme he had been searching for, the expression of what, consciously or unconsciously, he had always been working towards – security printing. His playing cards were already one form of such printing – in so far as every card in the pack must identically resemble the others. His 'Calico' invention, using a Jacquard loom to create 'a cloth of wires', enabled him to produce the criss-cross lines 'like the checks of tartan' for the repetitive, all-over patterns of playing card backs, and ultimately for all kinds of security printing. 'Mr de la Rue is prouder of his wire cloth invention than for any other improvements he may have introduced', wrote *Chambers' Edinburgh Journal*. And well he might be, since the art of security printing supplied his house with its *raison d'être* for the whole of the next century.

It is possible that Thomas actually met Joseph Jacquard, the French inventor of the aforesaid loom, on one of his visits to Paris. Jacquard's dates were 1752 – 1834. It is more likely, certainly more typical of Thomas, that he absorbed the idea of the loom through a family connection, in this instance his future son-in-law and partner, Isaac James. In De La Rue's account books for July 1842, there appears this item: 'wire weaving Dr to Isaac James Looms for weaving wire now in use by Wm Brown at Spitalfields'. Isaac James is known to have been long domiciled in France; during his years in London he could have been acting as English agent for Jacquard looms. If such was the case he was certainly responsible for bringing the Jacquard machine to Thomas's notice.

\*     \*     \*

Twenty years were to elapse before De La Rue printed their first banknote, and fourteen before their first adhesive postage stamp. Their first Post Office envelopes, on the other hand, were to occur very soon. Warren had recently begun to strike up an acquaintanceship which was to ripen into an extremely influential association; his new friend was called Edwin Hill. He had a brother, an ex-schoolmaster turned Civil Servant, whose hobby horse was Post Office reform. His name was Rowland.

As every stamp-collecting schoolboy knows, in 1840 Rowland Hill was responsible for the introduction of prepaid Penny Postage into England. Before his day the pre-payment of letters was a matter of choice – the writer as often as not choosing to allow his recipient to foot the bill. The urgent need for the re-adjustment of this system is said to have occurred to Rowland Hill when the case was brought to his notice of an illiterate woman, whose literate son had emigrated to Australia. Year after year he wrote to his mother. Year after year his letters reached her in England, but she did not accept them. Why should she pay for a receipt stamp? As she could not read she would have been forced to employ a professional reader. In any case she was already aware of the one fact she really wanted to know. From the very existence of each letter it was clear that her son was alive, and well enough to write to her.

A Government Commission digested Rowland Hill's proposals for overcoming these abuses. In June 1839 Lord John Russell told the House of Commons of its findings. The Commission had recommended that Hill's proposition be accepted, and consequently he moved that the Government should issue Post Office envelopes. A competition held to decide the best design for these was won by William Mulready, R.A.

Mulready's envelopes were made of a thread paper produced by John Dickinson & Co. His own fanciful drawing was on the outside. A London daily published a description of this design depicting an assortment of 'Indian missionaries, elephants, packed and ready to start . . . a little terrier dog inquisitively gliding between the legs of the mysterious conclave . . . and a dutiful boy reading to his anxious mamma an account of her husband's hopeless shipwreck who, with hands clasped is blessing Rowland Hill for the cheap rate at which she gets the intelligence'. Fortunately for De La Rue, 'Mulreadies' were not a success, but envelopes, as such, were here to stay.

Hitherto it had been the practice to fold over one's sheet of writing-paper oneself, tucking the ends into each other somewhat chancily, and writing the address on the outside of the sheet. The advantages of a separate envelope were obvious. Surely, thought De La Rue, the eventual money lay in producing not only note-paper but what Rowland Hill described as 'those little paper bags called envelopes'.

Hill's other innovations included stamped envelopes and adhesive 'labels' or 'stamps' to be affixed to plain envelopes. But these, he was inclined to think, would not be satisfactory; he supposed they would be inclined to rub off. For De La Rue Rowland Hill was the man of the hour. Through his friendship with the Hill family, Warren was able to hang on the great man's words. He learned that he should leave 'labels' or 'stamps' alone for the moment, and concentrate on envelopes. 'Stamps' could always be worked upon at a later date, if and when they had proved themselves.

The increase in letter writing brought about by Penny Postage, with its uniform costs and more frequent deliveries, together with the general wane of illiteracy caused, as one Victorian journalist put it, 'the introduction of many new auxiliaries to epistolary correspondence'.

By the end of the 1840s a million letters were being sent through the post every day, five-sixths of which were enclosed in envelopes 'and nearly an equal number used in private conveyance'. Tipped off by the powers that counted in the Post Office, De La Rue ignored the opportunity of producing the earliest adhesive stamps like the Penny Blacks, and joined the race to capture the market for envelopes and other 'auxiliaries to epistolary correspondence'. A whole new stationery world was opening up there and then.

At the same time the Hill family was quietly consolidating its position. Friend Edwin Hill was appointed Supervisor of Stamps at the end of 1840, a fact which cannot have decreased the amount of inside information available to Warren. Together Edwin and Warren worked off and on for the next four years upon an envelope making machine, locked up in a back room at Somerset House.

Originally envelopes were sold flat and unfolded. It was left to the customer to fold his own. Then at a later date they were sold cut and folded, processes which were performed painstakingly by hand. The new invention of Warren and Edwin enabled more envelopes to be cut mechanically in an hour than by a skilled worker in a whole day, and in so doing changed Thomas's playing-card house into a structure of a much firmer order.

\*     \*     \*

Whether Thomas cracked his whip too hard over his son's backroom efforts, or whether Warren disapproved of his relationship with the Hills being exploited too blatantly, we shall never know. What is certain is that during the four year gestation period of the envelope making machine, Warren withdrew himself from the parental umbrella, took a thousand pounds' worth of his capital from the business, and set up on his own as a 'Wholesale Stationer' in Artillery Place. For the period 1841 to 1842 he appeared in the *Street Directory* with that title and address. He returned to the fold in 1845. In that year he replaced his capital, and there were no

further references in the *Street Directory* to any separate establishment under his name.

It is interesting to notice that when Warren himself came to run
the business with William Frederick, both brothers were reluctant
to increase the number of Hills in De La Rue. William Frederick
wrote to Warren in Italy about pressure being brought to bear on
him by the Hills to take into the firm yet another relation of
Rowland's, Albert this time. The de la Rue brothers gave in and
offered him a post at £200 a year, but only after they had taken
pains to point out that the appointment was not permanent and
'should be confined', as William Frederick said, 'to matters which
will not give him anything to do with Stamp Office work'.

\* \* \*

There was so much travelling salesmanship to be maintained that
Jonah Nathan could not handle it all, and part of the burden fell on
Warren, who journeyed all over England. Thomas was getting a
bargain in this eldest son, who seemed to be able to turn his hand
to anything. Not only was his inventiveness an asset, but also his
practical knowledge of the whole range of equipment used by the
firm. In its 1846 piece entitled 'A Day at De La Rue', *Chambers'
Edinburgh Journal* described the vast collection of steam engines
and machinery 'nestling in a cluster of old edifices' in Bunhill Row,
all supervised by Mr Warren de la Rue. 'This young gentleman',
says the journalist, 'mentioned to me that they could not possibly
conduct their business with satisfaction and profit unless they had
always ready at hand the means of repairing and making machinery; the time lost and trouble expended in getting this species of
work done out of the house would be ruinous'. Impressed by this
self-sufficiency the correspondent continued his tour, 'at length
descending to the drying room to which I was let down by an
apparatus called a "lift".'

When he was twenty-three Warren supervised the 'erection of
some large white lead works, the drawings for which he made

entirely himself'. He also invented a special boiler to make the men's tea, 'so constructed that the fine aroma of the tea is not lost'. At the times when he hankered after a purely scientific career, unfettered by the chores of business and the demands of his father, he could withdraw to a laboratory on the premises equipped 'with retorts, mixtures and a store of bottles sufficient to set up a chemist's shop and a chemical library of French and English books'. Partner Button, whose own establishment sold chemical apparatus, had been on hand to advise what to buy.

Only five years after Charles Button rescued them from the rocks the de la Rue family had expanded their stationery business into 'the largest establishment of its kind in the world' (*Chambers'*). By the mid forties they were selling a hundred thousand packs of cards annually. There were six other firms similarly employed; the nearest and longest-lived rival was Goodall (bought by De La Rue in 1921). These two firms together were producing two-thirds of all the playing cards in Great Britain.

\*     \*     \*

The aura of domesticity which surrounded Queen Victoria and her Consort spread down the social scale, and card playing was one of the pleasures which could be shared within the large Victorian family circle. The problem was how to win the lion's share of this growing playing-card market. One method, Thomas decided, was to administer regular doses of publicity at shrewdly spaced intervals. Three leading journals came out with major articles on De La Rue in 1842, 1846 and 1853. All of them were beneficial to the firm's good name. The journalists concerned were much taken with the family in Bunhill Row. Because these articles give us much contemporary detail it is worth taking a closer look at them. The first, *Bradshaw's* (price 1½d), published on April 16th 1842 an account entitled 'Visit to Messrs De La Rue's Card Factory', which, after heaping praises on the house for its ingenuity in modernising playing card production, gives a blow by blow account of

Thomas's new methods. As basically these still obtain the account is fascinating. First, says *Bradshaw's,* comes the preparation of the paper, which is subjected to pressure and brushed with white enamel to give it a highly polished finish. Then follows the printing of the playing-card fronts; these are divided into two groups, the 'pips', i.e. the numbered cards, and the 'têtes', i.e. the court cards. The pips are comparatively simple to print: 'Sets of blocks are produced, each containing forty engravings of one card, and as the ordinary method of letter press printing is employed, forty impressions of one card are obtained at the same moment. As the pips bear but one colour, black or red, they are worked together at the hand press . . .'

The printing of court cards, continues *Bradshaw's,* is more difficult since they contain five colours. (This is where Thomas's patent comes into its own). 'The colours are printed separately and are made to fit into each other with great nicety . . . for this purpose a series of blocks is provided, which if united would form the figure intended to be produced. By printing successively from these blocks, the different colours fall into their proper places, and the whole process is completed. The printed fronts then go off to the drying rooms for three or four days'.

The backs are printed in the same way. Thomas's Jacquard 'calico' method is used to produce 'repetitive tartan and criss-cross patterns from a single block engraved with straight lines and printed in one colour, which is afterwards crossed with the same or any other colour by again laying the sheet on the block, so that the first lines cross the second printing at any required angle'.

Then the cards are given solidarity. Between the fronts and the backs are pasted two ordinary layers of paper. To be of an especially smooth quality, the paste employed, notes *Bradshaw's,* 'is cooled by steam, even the pasting performed with a large brush in a series of systematic movements is something of a work of art'. Three or four years were needed to become a master paster, who as early as 1840 could command the ample wage of £2 per week.

In quantities of four or five reams at a time the newly pasted sheets of cards are now subjected to the gradual but powerful pressure of a hydraulic press of one hundred tons, which is worked by a steam engine. Any air bubbles between the layers of pasteboard are thus expelled. Again the sheets are carefully hung up to dry to prevent their warping. More pressure is applied to flatten and polish them. *Bradshaw's* says that if special quality is desired the backs are waterproofed with varnish. Finally in order that each finished pasteboard card be of identical size, the sheets are cut into single cards with a big scissors apparatus. By laying up the cards on a long bench, a workman can make up into packs two hundred lots of cards simultaneously.

We also learn from *Bradshaw's* that the finest quality cards were called 'Moguls', the next best 'Harrys', and those with imperfections 'Highlanders'. Tradition has it that the finest, the Moguls, were so called after the Mogul emperors, Harrys were kings – after Henry VIII – and Highlanders were Princes – after Bonnie Prince Charlie.

To insure that the necessary duty – in 1840 a shilling a pack – had been paid, each ace of spades was printed in the Stamp Office at Somerset House. An account of the numbers of aces was kept there by the authorities.

'The whole of Messrs De La Rue's establishment', concludes the *Bradshaw's* reporter, 'is carried out in a manner perfectly unique. Steam power wherever practicable is applied to the various departments of the business'. As James Watt's invention was still in its youth, Warren de la Rue deserved this applause for being go-ahead.

*     *     *

From 1840 until 1856 playing cards remained the firm's chief money maker. They constituted a springboard for any new fields of activity that De La Rue might wish to enter. In any publicity concerning the firm Thomas and Warren tried to see that playing cards, their most lucrative product, received pride of place.

At this point we might consider what kind of public De La Rue was reaching through articles in current journals. William and Robert Chambers were the distinguished Scottish publishers responsible for an elaborate 1846 piece on the firm. Mr William Chambers expressed the Company's intention to provide goods.

'In such form and price as must suit the convenience of every man in the British Dominions . . . Every Saturday when the poorest labourer in the country draws his humble earnings he shall have it in his power to purchase a mean of healthful and agreeable mental instruction . . . For those who live in the hills and who cannot go to church I shall give pithy passages from the great British moralists . . . To the ladies and gentlemen of "the old school" I shall relate innumerable anecdotes not one of which they ever heard before'.

So well did the Chambers brothers nourish their *Journal* readers that the public appetite was greatly stimulated, and in accordance with the heavy demand for more and bigger helpings they added the *Repository* and the *Miscellany*. From Thomas's point of view this was the kind of publicity eminently to be desired. As such journalism reached into all classes of homes it was as effective as an advertisement on present day television, with the extra advantage of being an unsolicited testimonial.

In a way which bore no relation to its size, Thomas's house was starting to become a minor household word. In 1853 Charles Dickens literally made it so. By then heartily celebrated, with Oliver asking for more all round England, and two continents crying over little Nell, he had launched his own journal, *Household Words*. After visiting Bunhill Row he devoted six pages in one issue to an article called 'A Pack of Cards' in which he extolled the firm's excellence. After a promising beginning – 'Sir Roger de

Coverley sent a pack of cards to every cottager family on his estate every Christmas. Cards are in season and we propose to take a hand' – Dickens made no more quips, forgot his Christmas Carol-like opening, and settled down to a ponderous exposition of the history of playing cards and De La Rue's part in it. His social conscience lets fall one typically Dickensian comment. 'Let it not be here supposed that a man trifles away his life by sticking sheets of paper together'.

The backgrounds of Thomas de la Rue and his visitor, Charles Dickens, were not dissimilar; both had suffered financial misfortune. While Thomas was a child-apprentice to a printer, Dickens had stuck labels on bottles in a blacking factory, snatching spare moments to visit his father in the debtors' prison of the Marshalsea. He had cause to sympathise with Thomas's previous ups and downs, including his short sojourn in gaol.

\*     \*     \*

One move by the de la Rues which Dickens remarked on was the securing of Owen Jones's services to design playing-card backs. Owen Jones was a Welsh architect, who was to become well known for the illuminated giftbooks beloved by Victorians, and whose *Grammar of Ornamentation* came to be regarded as a masterpiece. He started working for Thomas in 1844, and in the ensuing twenty years created 173 different playing-card designs varying from fruit-and-flower themes to Chinese and Arabesque. Dickens was delighted with the 'dainty little pictures' by Owen Jones which appeared on the firm's playing cards for members of the Royal family. The Queen's were excessively *jeune fille*, all roses and hawthorn. Prince Albert's consisted mostly of prickly holly garnished with ivy and oak, while the poor Prince of Wales got girlish daises and fuschias. One would have thought that only the Princess Royal's primroses, violets and lilies were at all appropriate but, tactfully with Dickens, 'we will leave those who are learned in the language of flowers to interpret all these symbols and apply them to the proper objects'.[1]

Owen Jones played a prominent part in the lives of three generations of de la Rues – Thomas, assisting Warren and William Frederick, and finally Warren's son, the eccentric Warren William, who was sent to him to learn lithography. Although Thomas left Jones nothing in his will, William Frederick made the affectionate gesture of leaving him '£52 to buy something in remembrance of me', a pound for every card in a pack.

\*       \*       \*

*Chambers' Journal* had noted two side lines at De La Rue, which were natural offshoots from playing cards and involved no additional outlay. The first was railway tickets. In 1832 the Duke of Wellington, who was opening an early railway with a certain amount of misgiving, pondered the fact that this mode of transport 'enabled the lower classes to travel about needlessly'. A decade later they were moving about to such an extent that railway companies mushroomed, the colonnade at Euston station was declared the eighth wonder of the world, and Thomas jumped on the railway bandwagon. In 1841 he obtained his first order from the London and Blackwall Railway in whose account books appear the item: '25th April 1843 AGREED that cheques be drawn for the following payment. De La Rue & Co, for Passengers check tickets £39 2s 6d'. According to *Chambers'* by 1846 De La Rue were making the tickets for 'nearly all the railways in the United Kingdom', a profitable way of using up any odd pieces of pasteboard not wanted for playing cards. By 1856 they were making a million and a half tickets a week.

The other side line was visiting cards. In the eighteenth century Voltaire, having unsuccessfully called on an absent friend, 'sur une

[1] Jones-designed cards were expensive. De La Rue advertised the 'Royal Illuminated Playing Cards' in an 1851 *Illustrated London News* at 'Two Guineas the Set of four patterns or singly 10s 6d the pack'.

carte à jouer très sale' wrote crossly: 'M. de Voltaire est venu quatre fois'. After the fall of the Bastille citizens jotted down observations against each other on the backs of playing cards – and changed their court cards into heroes of the Revolution. (One king became Voltaire himself). Because playing cards could be conveniently carried upon the person, and did not crumple like ordinary notepaper, they were found to be handy for jotting down messages, a necessary improvement on the verbal messages of illiterate eighteenth century servants which got hopelessly garbled.

Thomas reduced the size of the cards, thereby rendering them more portable. He also employed his enamelled playing-card paper which bent less easily than the flimsier, pre-De La Rue cards. Apart from inventing the modern English playing card, for what such arbitrary titles are worth, Thomas could also be called 'the father of the English visiting card', or as *Chambers'* called it, 'the enamelled calling-card'.

*    *    *

On the foreign front a strange episode occurred in 1843. Thomas gained the entrée to the Court of the Tsar of all the Russias. He contrived to have his youngest brother, Paul, appointed superintendent of the Russian royal playing card making monopoly. Considering that Paul was minding the family millinery until only two years before, this was a peculiar achievement. Yet the appointment turned out to be a success. Paul held it for the rest of his working life.

The mind boggles at the thought of any connection at that date between Bunhill Row, EC1, and the Court of St Petersburg. But it is no discredit to Thomas's business acumen to point out that commercial relations between Russia and the rest of Europe were much closer than they are today. Her agents were all over the place, and her trading outlook was cosmopolitan. Whereas the language of the Court was French, Russia's business affairs tended to be conducted by Germans.

5. The Five Cents Blue (The 'London Print') made by De La Rue for the Confederate States of America, and shipped to North Carolina, November 1862. The stamp bears the head of Jefferson Davis

The first banknote to be printed by De La Rue for Mauritius in 1860

Asserting

Miss Dram the Doctor's Daugh[...]

for little brother

Miss Dram the Doctor's Daug[...]

6. De La Rue card games of the 1890s

Yet with such international competition it is all the more remarkable that in October 1842, Paul Bienvenu de la Rue found himself travelling to St Petersburg with £150 of the firm's money in his pocket book 'to take entire charge of Russian playing card manufacture'.

The Marquis de Custine, who made the same journey at the same time, quotes a Lübeck innkeeper as saying 'they (the Russians) have two expressions . . . when they come through here on the way to Europe they have a gay, free, happy air. They are like horses turned out to pasture . . . the same people on their return have long gloomy, tormented faces'. Arriving in time for the worst of the winter, Paul could wonder whether Tsar Nicholas I's cousin, Queen Victoria, was right in attributing the reactionary spirit in Russia to 'the terribly unhealthy atmosphere caused by keeping their windows battened down from September to May'.

A typically resilient product of his family, Paul took such hazards in his stride. He moved in an international circle in St Petersburg, where his best friends were American. As a foreigner he did not suffer the constraint endured by Russian society in which it was unsafe to utter an opinion on anything other than social chit-chat.

The stranglehold of Tsarist despotism affected the playing-card business. In the provinces, as well as in the capital, with the early dark, and the day's work over by four 'recourse is almost invariably had to card playing which is indulged in to an extent that we have no conception of in England . . . It is no unusual thing for gentlemen to play for eight or nine hours at a time . . . At the weekly club dinners, before coffee has been served, nearly all present used to rush off impatiently to the card-table'. The Russians were the biggest playing-card customers in Europe, and got through a million packs of cards a year. No wonder the Tsar cast envious glances at the profits going into the pockets of other countries, and prohibited imports. *Chambers' Journal* believed

Thomas's assurance that the proceeds of the Russian playing-card monopoly were devoted to charitable purposes. But the Marquis de Custine, more sceptical, noted that most financial transactions seemed destined to swell the Tsar's private coffers, including a change in the value of the rouble itself, a measure which recently brought in the exact amount needed to rebuild the Winter Palace.

Communication was difficult. The Marquis de Custine did not dare post home one word against the regime all the time he was in Russia. Thomas may well have been oblivious of the despotic state of Tsarist affairs. In any case they were not his concern. He merely went so far as to say that the Tsar paid him 'with much liberality' for divulging his playing-card making expertise. His Imperial Majesty, on his side, had reason to be satisfied with the results of the negotiations with De La Rue. Thomas gave such good advice, his brother Paul managed affairs so ably, that by 1847, four years after his arrival on the scene, the production by the Tsarist monopoly had been stepped up from one to four million packs a year, making it easily the biggest playing-card plant in the world. Total English playing-card production did not pass the million mark till 1873.

A year to the month after Paul's arrival a roller press (at a cost of £130) was sent, as promised, from Bunhill Row to St Petersburg (packing £11 5s) and De La Rue supplied machinery, inks and paper for manufacturing the Tsar's playing cards. The sale of these commodities on a large scale meant that the Russian establishment, with Paul as manager, was a considerable customer of De La Rue. This was the firm's first overseas trade.

Pre-eminent among Paul's circle of friends in St Petersburg were a family from Baltimore, U.S.A., called Winans, who were busy seeing to the building of the Trans-Siberian Railway. According to family legend the fortune they amassed in the process was considerably increased by the flamboyant gesture of the Tsar, who threw down his ruler across the map of Russia, demanding that the railroad follow a similarly straight line. Sensibly the Winans's charged the earth for surmounting the difficulties, thereby making their millions.

Paul's daughter, Maria Ann de la Rue, married the millions in the person of Walter Winans, son of the head of the family, Ross Winans. The wedding in St Petersburg was attended by leading embassy officials. It is doubtful whether she would have made such a brilliant match had she never moved out of Finsbury.

Maria Ann's father-in-law, Ross Winans, had his own bearing on the story of De La Rue. Although he lived in the North throughout the American Civil War, he was one of the most outstanding of all Confederate supporters. Suspected of wishing to deliver his vast supply of railway rolling-stock to the Confederacy, he was twice imprisoned for his sympathies. In Maryland, where Southern Confederate sympathizers had a strong nucleus of support, he was commissioned to manufacture arms. He himself designed a revolving cannon powered by steam. A member of the Maryland legislature, a man of great wealth and influence, he knew everyone of importance in his day.

When William Frederick set off for America about the time of the Winans-de la Rue nuptials, he went armed with this family introduction. Ross Winans's prominence in Confederate army circles would explain, for instance, how his young cousin by marriage, William Frederick de la Rue, later came to be presented with a piece of the flag-staff at Fort Sumter by the Confederate hero, General Beauregard.

Such connections were of assistance to William Frederick in his subsequent negotiations with the Confederate States, resulting in the firm's printing of the Blue and the Orange Confederate stamps, which are renowned in the philatelic world. Of these we shall hear more. For the moment let us record that the chance romance in St Petersburg between a de la Rue girl and a boy from Baltimore led to a dramatic business development in Bunhill Row, London.

Apart from de la Rue family relationships in the States, partner Jonah Nathan had a useful American connection in Louis Cohen, a leading New York playing card maker who shared the services of designer Owen Jones. With the assistance of these contacts William Frederick was able to do some useful reconnaissance work. As a result De La Rue opened a New York office even before they had one in Paris. The Parisian office was not established until 1863, nearly a decade later.

# CHAPTER V

# Framework and scaffolding

Back in Bunhill Row Thomas was changing partners yet again. In 1844 Charles Button returned to his underwater cables, confident that his young protegé, Warren, was established in a secure family business.

Mr Button was to be the last outsider; all future partners were de la Rues, or old faithfuls like the scholarly Augustus Fry and the diligent Jonah Nathan, both of whom were now permitted to join the partnership. While Mr Fry was supporting Thomas with forbearance in the legal battles of the 1830s, Mr Nathan, as senior traveller, had been loyally working his way round England, gaining the lasting respect of 'the trade' and keeping De La Rue alive through the lean years. He belonged to a prosperous Jewish family of quillmakers, who took as armorial bearings an appropriate 'shield Azure three pens in fesse Argent'.

*   *   *

The firm began to specialise in the fancy stationery dear to the Victorian taste. It also profited by the fact that it was an age of elaborate eating, and printed exquisitely embellished menus on pale satins describing gargantuan bills of fare. A choice of fourteen entrées, four hot and ten cold, was not unusual. Louis Eustache Ude, the celebrated chef at Crockfords, who listed printing and engraving amongst his other interests, made the irrefutable comment: 'If you have eaten too much doubtless you will feel inconvenienced'. In order that guests might revive in time to read the next menu he suggested 'immediate recourse to some weak tea'.

69

In the first half of the nineteenth century letter-writing was considered an accomplishment of consequence. It was one of the occupations which ladies might use with propriety to fill their day – the gentlemen were useful for sharpening the quills. As the fashion in stationery became more elaborate, De La Rue found one of their best sellers was a *papeterie* containing assorted notepapers. There was a wealth of etiquette attached to the kind of notepaper one used. Mourning paper, for example, was *de rigueur* upon the demise of all relatives, the size of the border depending on their nearness and standing. After the death of the Prince Consort Queen Victoria always used mourning notepaper, some of it supplied by De La Rue.

Towards the end of the forties, the paraphernalia of Mid-Victoriana was snowballing into production in Bunhill Row in the form of silver wedding cards, lace edged and coloured notepapers, and memorandum cards with pithy sayings like the punctuality card designed by Thomas's old partner, William Frederick Rock: 'METHOD is the sole support of BUSINESS and there is no METHOD without PUNCTUALITY. *Punctuality is important* Because it Subserves the Peace and Good Order of a Family'.

While the numerous members of Victorian households awaited their turn to sit at the escritoire, William Frederick de la Rue was trying to relieve their plight by designing a portable writing-desk, which could be comfortably placed on one's knees. At the same time Warren was hard at work putting the finishing touches to the envelope making machine. He improved on the earlier invention, made in collaboration with Edwin Hill. His new machine not only cut and folded the envelopes, but gummed them as well.

The reason for this extra activity at De La Rue was the edifice sketched on William Paxton's drawing board – Prince Albert's Crystal Palace. As yet the very idea of it was being laughed at, but to the accompaniment of Queen Victoria's pride and satisfaction, the Consort eventually had his way. The rush to prepare for the

1851 Exhibition was on, and the de la Rues were in the thick of it.

*    *    *

The year before the Great Exhibition opened, Warren, already a leading member of the Royal Chemical Society, was elected to the Royal Society. The most august body in London, the haunt of Prince Albert, the platform of amateur scientists like Lord Northampton, and professionals like Michael Faraday, the Society was an integral part of Warren's life for the rest of his days. He lived long enough to be its Secretary, but missed occupying the lofty position of its Presidency, his one secret ambition.

At a contemporary conversazione, given to the Fellows of the Royal Society by the royal Duke of Sussex, the guests were 'the most distinguished in science, literature and rank'. In one room Michael Faraday was showing an experiment in electro magnetism, watched by the ageing Talleyrand. In another Lord Brougham and the Bishops of London and Worcester were holding forth. A Royal Society soirée was 'attended by a numerous assembly of *savants* and of the nobility. Prince Albert, accompanied by his cousins now on a visit to the Queen, arrived soon after nine. H.R.H., for upwards of half an hour, inspected various objects by the microscope . . .' On such an occasion Warren could not help being to the fore. Faraday was his friend, whom he assisted by placing his private laboratories at his disposal.

Warren's fellowship of the Royal Society was important to De La Rue. It enabled him to meet the eminences not only of the English, but also of the European, scientific scene. Through the Society's auspices he was able to find and employ so distinguished a man as Dr Hugo Müller of Leipzig, who, apart from the de la Rue family, was to make a deeper impression on the firm than anyone else in the nineteenth century.

The timing of Warren's election was splendid. In one way or another, from Prince Albert downwards, the planning of the 1851 Exhibition was dominated by Fellows of the Society. The two stalwarts on whom the Prince Consort most relied to launch his schemes were both well-known to the de la Rues: Henry Cole, Fellow of the Royal Society, together with none other than the firm's own designer, Owen Jones. The latter was appointed superintendent of works. In a burst of exuberance he planned to paint the 'underside of every girder red, the round portions of the columns yellow, and the concaves and hollows blue'. *The Times* protested loudly, but in vain.

With these contacts it is possible to understand the prominence achieved by De La Rue in Hyde Park, a prominence which was remarkable considering that only a decade had elapsed since the firm was verging on bankruptcy.

Henry Cole and his committees, upon several of which sat Thomas and Warren, struggled with international requests. They dissuaded the Swiss, says Mr Christopher Hobhouse, from sending cheeses, and attended to the parcel from France addressed to 'Sir Vyatt and Sir Fox Enderson Esq, Grate Exposition, Park of Hide at London, Glace softly to be posed upright'. America sent a 'mammoth double action grand pianoforte to be used by three or four performers simultaneously', and some 'collapsible bedsteads impervious to vermin'. A speciality from Pennsylvania was a Buck-eyed squirrel (stuffed). From Philadelphia came false teeth. The list from the entire North American continent, however, was short compared with the 289 items listed by De La Rue. They had the distinction of having every single one printed in the Exhibition catalogue, the only stand to do so.

The Crystal Palace housed the most heterogeneous collection of objects ever gathered under one roof, and provided an unprecedented shopwindow to the world. If De La Rue had been publicity-conscious before, they surpassed themselves now. They procured the most advantageous site available in the central aisle of the English exhibition. The *pièce de résistance* of their stand was the envelope making machine in full operation.

It drew tremendous crowds. 'None other', wrote the *Illustrated London News*, 'can boast of bigger congregations . . . There are few things in fact which Paxton's glass shade contains more attractive to the curious than this'. Journalists of other countries added their compliments. The *Illustrierte Zeitung* of Leipzig described its folding and gumming processes, observing that the machine could be run by 'one boy or one maid', and 'can always attract inquisitive persons to whom the finished envelopes are generously distributed'.

A guide book called *The Crystal Palace and its Contents* made the graphic comment that 'the inventors of the machine have closely followed the several movements of the human frame, the cams especially exhibiting their thorough knowledge of animal mechanics'. A later edition of the *Illustrated London News* has a picture of the De La Rue stand: in this, beneath a notice requesting visitors not to touch, a crinolined lady peruses a catalogue while her elegant escort stares stonily into the distance. Left foreground a stout party in a paisley shawl restrains a child who points in wonder at the envelope making machine.

Grouped around the De La Rue stand were items varying from 'Ladies' 14 inch Double Desk with Plated Silver Handles and Hinges, Bound in Green Calf, richly Blind Tooled, Ladies' Purple ditto' to 'EXPANDING SERMON CASES' for expansive Victorian sermons. There was a 'Pocket Chess Board Complete' originated by Roget of the 'Thesaurus', who was the Secretary of the Royal Society, plus playing cards with pips in different colours for short-sighted people, an idea suggested to the de la Rues by Sir Frankland Lewis. As Joint Secretary of the Treasury, Sir Frankland was in the Rowland Hill circle. He is said to have been a 'careful and accomplished man but formal, verbose and dull'. The playing cards inspired by him turned out to be one of De La Rue's few current failures.

73

The official catalogue of the Exhibition reserved one of its biggest write-ups for the envelope making machine. Its report on the latter is worthy of Beachcomber's Dr Strabismus (whom God preserve of Utrecht) who might have used it to describe his device for getting the fluff out of ferrets' ears:

'A plunger now descends and creases the envelope by carrying it between the folder axes, at the same time turning the flaps upwards in a vertical direction. The plunger which descended as a whole, now divides into two parts, the ends rising and the sides remaining to hold the envelope until the end folders have operated . . . the envelopes are now knocked over on to an endless blanket and are conducted between two cylinders for a final squeeze . . .' In one hour this operation produced 2,700 envelopes.

Frivolously the cataloguer falls to wondering what all these envelopes will contain:

'In illustration of the things sometimes sent by post it may be cited that some years back Professor Henslow was in the habit of receiving from members of an agricultural society specimens of living slugs of various kinds'.

*　　*　　*

Such was the fame enjoyed by the envelope making machine at the 1851 Exhibition that other establishments began to make use of it. The largest advertisement in the *Morning Herald* of June 6th 1851 was that inserted on the front page by Hyam & Co. of Oxford Street, Tailors and Clothiers, headed: 'THE EXPANDING FIGURE OF THE GREAT EXHIBITION'. This, it transpired, was the envelope making machine. 'However successful this invention may prove', Hyam & Co. claimed confidently, 'in measurement it will after all be "measure for measure" when placed in comparison with the fit of our own durable, wellmade, fashionable and cheap specimens of gentlemen's attire'.

*　　*　　*

Thomas and Warren were both appointed Jurors of the Exhibition, which meant they were on the prize-awarding panels. Fair play throughout being the order of the day, royal command had decreed that the chairman and jurors for each class should be half British and half foreign. Thus in the case of Class 17 (Paper, Stationery, Printing and Bookbinding) the chairman was H.E. The Belgian Ambassador, Sylvain van der Weyer. The deputy chairman was Thomas de la Rue, who had moved from Bunhill Row to the more fashionable and suitably adjacent address of 84 Westbourne Terrace, Hyde Park. Lesser members of the committee were Professor Hulse, Director of the Royal Polytechnical Academy at Dresden, M. Didot, Printer to the Institute of France, and Lord Mahon, yet another Fellow of the Royal Society.

The jurors of Class 17 unanimously passed a resolution regretting that 'the position of Mr de la Rue as a juror has not allowed the jury to recommend that the Council Medal be awarded to him, which in their opinion he so justly deserves'. Not that Thomas cared. He had it both ways. He received instead a special medal, presented by a commission presided over by the Prince Consort, for his services rendered to the Exhibition as a whole.

He also got a bronze medal for his invention of iridescent film which the jurors thought was 'a beautiful illustration of the production of colour on a thin transparent surface such as is transiently seen in an ordinary soap bubble'.

The House received a Bronze Medal for the excellence of its complete exhibit, another for the envelope making machine, and Warren also collected a medal for his juror work. The jurors' reports sang the firm's praises to an embarrassing degree: 'Messrs De La Rue & Co. as paper finishers displayed every description of the best writing papers produced in England. The mode of perforating thick paper and cardboard was first applied by Monsieur Marc La Rivière, a Swiss watch-maker . . . but Mr de la Rue suggested its application to paper and cardboard'. They mentioned briefly that Messrs Waterlow also had an envelope folding machine, but added deprecatingly that it was 'patented by M. Remond some years after that of Messrs De La Rue & Co'.

The year of concentrated effort in Bunhill Row had been worth it. The Great Exhibition was a resounding success for the House. It covered itself with honours, and individual de la Rues established themselves as authorities in their fields. In addition the international and national publicity surpassed all expectation. A profound significance of the Crystal Palace was the precedent created by the inter-mingling of social classes. 110,000 visitors came on a single day. The unsophisticated masses poured in from the countryside on the new railways. They came into contact with the machine age, an experience 'which moved the strongest to tears'. At the other end of the scale the Great Exhibition set off a chain of subsequent royal visits round De La Rue which has continued through every reign into the present day.

So pleased were the de la Rue family with the outcome that they bought the picture by Henry Selous of the Exhibition's opening by the Queen. Thomas is on the righthand side, Warren in the background. On Warren's death, Warren William de la Rue presented the picture to the Victoria and Albert Museum.

*     *     *

To close the 1851 saga a short and hilarious sequel remains to be reported. In August the city of Paris, says Miss Yvonne ffrench, fêted all the most important English people connected with the Great Exhibition. From the start the visit was a farcical disaster. Guests of honour Sir Henry and Lady Cole arrived at Victoria Station in time to see the special train going out. When they eventually got to Paris they found that in common with two-thirds of their fellow guests their baggage had not only been left behind at Boulogne, but had been thoughtfully sent back to England by the French customs. Only Thomas de la Rue seems to have landed with his luggage reasonably intact. At any rate he was able to lend his clothes around Paris – Sir Henry Cole said he borrowed Thomas's 'huge pair of black trousers which were double my cubic capacity'. In the matter of accommodation, also, Thomas came to the rescue. He pulled enough strings at the Meurice Hotel to enable the poor, stranded Coles at least to have 'a little room to be in'.

    \*        \*        \*

By the time of the New York and Paris exhibitions in 1853 and 1855, De La Rue were experienced exhibitors. In New York, where they were awarded prize medals for diaries, calendars and vegetable parchment, they appear to have expended the comparatively modest sum of £89 12s 4d on their stand. But two years later at the Paris exhibition, they spent £1,000 by instalments, won two gold, two silver and two bronze medals, and Thomas was made a Chevalier d'Honneur.

# CHAPTER VI

# The ground floor:
# Thomas, Warren and Colonel Billy

When the excitement of the Great Exhibition had died down, the de la Rues took stock of themselves. Thomas was approaching sixty. There was plenty of fire left in him yet, as he was shortly to prove, but nevertheless he felt that the partnership needed new energies. His second son, twenty-five year old William Frederick, was engaged to be married. As he had done for Warren, by way of a wedding gift, Thomas made William Frederick a partner too, and put up a thousand pounds for his share of the capital.

After joining the volunteer regiment of the 4th Tower Hamlets, William Frederick was usually known as 'Colonel Billy'. During the early fifties there was an upsurge of patriotic feeling in a Britain closely watching Napoleon III after his *coup d'état*. People were still mindful of the first Napoleon. With characteristic lack of fuss William Frederick speedily offered his services to the Militia, financing the 4th Tower Hamlets for some years from his own purse, and organizing its affairs in such free time as he had.

He has been described as 'an Elizabethan born out of his age, with the charm that overcomes obstacles both human and material – the Cavalier as well as the Colonel'. In a family already noted for its charm, his was the most irresistible of all; spiked with a caustic wit, it was quite spontaneous. Its effect in business was powerful. If Warren, who was considered 'a diplomatist of the highest order', lent 'tact . . . and suavity of manner' to the De

La Rue partnership, his younger brother contributed breezy authority combined with bonhomie.

Like Thomas himself, Colonel Billy was put to work early. We caught a glimpse of him as a twelve year old, helping out in Bunhill Row during the financial crisis. After his fifteenth birthday he became a traveller for De La Rue, and Thomas kept him continuously on the road. Although he was so young he was responsible for selling thousands of pounds worth of playing cards and stationery. Like his father he was schooled by the rough and tumble of business, rather than by scholastic institutions.

In spite of the ten-year age gap between Warren and Colonel Billy, and the difference in their education, the younger brother was in no way overawed by the elder. Colonel Billy's eagle eye missed little in Bunhill Row, nor did it overlook an opportunity to pull his eminent brother's leg. 'Your telegram of the 17th was utterly unintelligible', he wired Warren in Italy: 'you did not say where you were staying . . . we first thought you had been captured by brigands and that £50 was your ransom money'. At the same time he could write to him solicitously: 'I hope you will not hurry back while you are enjoying yourselves. All is going well and I want you to have a good stock of health when you do come back. I think you were not looking well in Paris'. Their understanding was so close that they could switch positions effortlessly. Colonel Billy took charge in London when Warren was abroad or scientifically engaged, and Warren resumed the reins when his brother was away on a selling mission. It was the ideal partnership.

1850 had been Colonel Billy's busy year. Apart from helping with the Great Exhibition preparations, going to North America, and being made a partner, he had arrangements to make for his forthcoming wedding to Emma Tanner, the daughter of a well-to-do family who lived in Charterhouse Square. He had left his parents' home some time before, preferring to live with Warren and Georgiana in Canonbury. When his parents moved out of their house in Bunhill Row to live in the West End, Colonel Billy took it over for his bride.

He was always 'on call' there. A report to Edwin Hill in 1856 states that 'Mr William de la Rue, whose house adjoins the office, would undertake the safe custody of the die in the night'. By 1864 Colonel Billy and Emma had had enough of living so close to the business. They moved their family up to fashionable Harley Street, and became the first of a colony of De La Rue partners and directors to live near Regent's Park.

*    *    *

Warren was beginning to reach impressive heights in scientific circles, particularly on the subject of astronomy. He built an observatory onto his Canonbury House and then, outgrowing this, bought a property at Cranford, Middlesex where he installed a bigger observatory, with a reflecting telescope made to his design. A daguerreotype of the moon, taken by an American, and exhibited at the Crystal Palace, fired his imagination. He started to devise his own methods of lunar photography.

His advice was also increasingly sought on commercial affairs. When Lyon Playfair, the organizer of the juries for the Great Exhibition, was appointed Secretary of the Science and Art department at South Kensington in 1853, he wrote immediately to Warren from Marlborough House asking his confidential opinion about the state of the paper trade in England. As one might expect, Warren spent a month doing intensive research, and then sent back a comprehensive survey with some interesting conclusions. 'It would appear', he wrote, 'that railways and steam boats consume a very large quantity of waste for wiping machinery which formerly found its way to the paper mill. But the most important of all competitors are undoubtedly the Americans who of late years have purchased largely in our own market . . .' He points out that 'the growing thirst after literature' is increasing the demand for paper and advises that 'new fibrous materials' will have

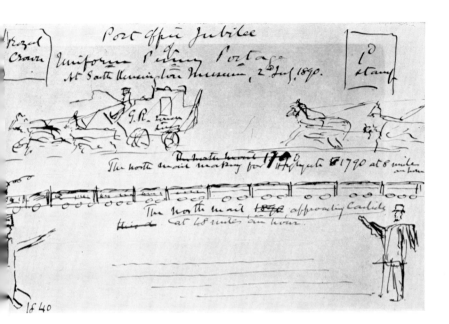

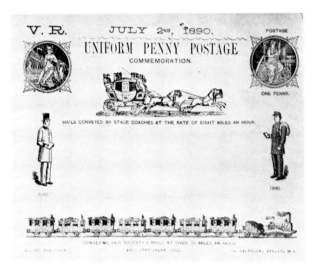

Preliminary sketch, and finished envelope, made by De La Rue and issued by the Post Office in 1890 to celebrate the fiftieth anniversary of Penny Postage

8. George Sweetser, designer of the Onoto pen, *left* as a female impersonator on roller skates, *right* as an octogenarian, still roller-skating vigorously

to be found to augment the traditional materials of rags for paper production. As early as the 1840s De La Rue themselves were getting through 45,000 reams of paper a year. Warren set about enquiring into a possible shortage. He and Professor A. W. Hofmann, Fellow of the Royal Society, experimented with vegetable parchment, which Professor Hofmann found greatly superior in strength to real parchment, being 'capable of resisting the tooth of time for many centuries'.

\*     \*     \*

Thomas and sons were standing on the threshold of the most exciting developments in their house's history. Originally Rowland Hill had had no faith in the future of adhesive stamps. In the months following the Great Exhibition, however, he began to think otherwise. In April 1853, the Board of Inland Revenue decided to use adhesive fiscal stamps on drafts and receipts. As there was no room to produce them at Somerset House, the de la Rues were awarded a four year contract to make them in Bunhill Row.

This was heady news for the firm. For one thing the Government had *not* approached Perkins Bacon & Co., the makers of the first postage stamps (including the Penny Black and Twopenny Blue). More sensational still, the Board of Inland Revenue decided to risk letting the de la Rues print the fiscal stamps by their new typographical process, the same one that Thomas had used for his playing cards. The Hills had heard sufficient in private about De La Rue inventions, and seen enough of them in public at the Great Exhibition, to justify the experiment.

The Perkins Bacon stamps were line engraved, a process by which every sheet was hand printed from a transferred plate. It produced superlative stamps at a disproportionately high cost. The De La Rue improved typographical, or surface printed, method was more practical. First, claimed the de la Rues, because of special fugitive ink which disappeared when fraudulent persons attempted to clean the stamps for use a second time, their method could prevent Post Office losses, a problem 'about which the Board was always nervous'. Secondly, they claimed that their treatment of stamp paper was better suited to perforation. Here they trod on an Achilles heel because Perkins Bacon had had a lot of perforation troubles; their paper often shrank after the damping necessary for line-engraved printing, and then did not fit satisfactorily in the perforating machine at Somerset House. De La Rue were not proposing to damp the paper at all.

Sir Henry Cole also pointed out that the De La Rue stamps were more economical 'than those first invented . . . to the extent it is said of £10,000 a year'. Sir Rowland Hill, pressed by the Chancellor of the Exchequer to increase Post Office revenue to help pay for the Crimean War, found the idea of this potential saving very attractive.

From the de la Rues' point of view, the Government's new interest in surface printed stamps was timely. They themselves felt they had gone as far in the playing card field as it was possible to go; they were ahead of their competitiors in home and foreign sales. Also as 'Cavendish' (the card-game expert) commented, there was a current decline in the number of aces being registered at Somerset House. This falling off was largely due to an illegal trade being conducted in slightly damaged cards, or 'seconds', which were not liable to duty. Firms like De La Rue, who prided themselves on perfection, could not afford to be involved. Later in 1862, the Government was forced to reduce the tax on playing cards from one shilling to threepence a pack, but well before this the Company had found more important things to do. It was convinced that the same process that made playing cards could also make stamps.

\*     \*     \*

In December 1853, De La Rue sent the Board of Inland Revenue a bill for £1,013 0s 7d for their work on the fiscal stamps. Included was the item: 'outlay for new premises £677 4s 6d'. This was meticulously reduced by a third to £225 14s 10d 'as part of the fittings are applicable to this purpose only'. The Board thought the cost so reasonable and the stamps so satisfactory that only a few days after De La Rue sent in their bill for them, Rowland Hill's son, Ormond, wrote to Jean Ferdinand de la Ferté enclosing 'the drawings of H.M. head which we wish to have engraved . . . Our object as you are aware is to obtain in hardened steel a cut or engraving of this head and ground fitted for surface printing . . .' The surface printing here referred to was to be performed by De La Rue, the object being none other than the production of their first postage stamp, the famous Fourpenny Carmine, issued in 1855. Made of an ink described as 'purest Carmine', the De La Rue Fourpenny has been regarded with reverence in the world of philately ever since.

Its designer, Joubert de la Ferté, the last of the great French line engravers, came to London in 1842 to marry an English girl called Amelia Bennett. He enjoyed a measure of success in this country; his own paintings were exhibited at the Royal Academy, and subsequently the Joubert-De La Rue association blossomed as stamp business boomed. Between 1855 and 1877 Joubert designed over twenty issues of postage and fiscal stamps for the Company.

&ast;  &ast;  &ast;

The pace was beginning to warm up. De La Rue also started printing stamps for the East India Company. Unfortunately the Bunhill Row records concerning the East India Company contracts perished in the London blitz, and only one letter survives, written to the de la Rues from East India House on the 14th October 1854. It begins:

'Gentlemen,

The Court of Directors of the East India Company have had before them your offer to supply annually for five years, the requisite quantity of thirty five millions of Postage Labels for India at the

rate of One shilling and sixpence per thousand . . . I am commanded to inform you that the Court has accepted the said
offer . . .' The 'postage labels' referred to were the four anna and
eight anna stamps. The early association with the East India
Company heralded a large and lasting business for De La Rue.
Within a few years the firm was supplying the whole sub-continent with all postal requirements, including vast quantities of
Governmental stationery.

\*     \*     \*

In addition to the East India Company stamps, De La Rue received
a minute in July 1855 from the Board of Inland Revenue instructing
them to prepare 'forms for One shilling and Sixpenny postage
labels'. The One Shilling Green and Sixpenny Lilac were issued
the following year. The fact that the de la Rues knew so many
Hills in and around the Board of Inland Revenue, however, did not
necessarily ensure that the firm received favoured treatment. Just
after the appearance of the shilling and sixpenny stamps the
G.P.O. suddenly became apprehensive about the Fourpenny
Carmine's 'facility of removal' (i.e. the possibility of its being
cleaned and re-used). That the excellence of the Carmine, their
pride and joy, should be challenged astonished the de la Rues.
They sprang to its defence and plunged Bunhill Row into a series
of exhaustive experiments to prove that the house had 'produced
a stamp as perfectly secure as possible against re-issue'.

The account of £164 which they rendered for their efforts made
no charge for 'Mr de la Rue and Mr Warren de la Rue's time and
superintendence'. Unimpressed by this concession, the Board
loftily expected all such work to be included in the original price
for no extra charge whatsoever, and repeated that it did not feel
justified in paying the additional expenses of 'experiments made
by you in order to enable you to perform your engagements in a
satisfactory manner'.

In spite of a strong recommendation by Ormond Hill that the

Government bear two-thirds of the cost of the De La Rue experiments, and the firm one-third, the Board refused to pay a penny. The refusal illustrates the toughness of the Inland Revenue. Since De La Rue were ultimately able to satisfy this most exacting of customers with such completeness, it is not surprising that other Governments followed suit and placed their stamp-printing orders in Bunhill Row.

\*    \*    \*

With their surface printed stamps the firm began to lead the field. Thomas's resounding words, noted down by Mr Chambers's correspondent, took on a new significance: 'Competition with others won't do any longer. The true art consists in not waiting to be stimulated by rivalry . . .' It was Warren's determination not to wait which gave De La Rue their lead in security printing. From now on business and pleasure proceeded for him in an agreeable combination. There were so many printing experiments upon which he wanted to embark in Bunhill Row that he asked his friends in the Royal Society if they could recommend anyone to help him. The distinguished scientist Baron Liebig magnanimously sent him the name of one of his own assistants, a promising Bavarian chemist called Hugo Müller.

According to the *Transactions of the Chemical Society*, from the moment of his arrival in England Hugo Müller fell under Warren de la Rue's spell. 'The unformed, simple young German, for such he was, it is said, when he came here, could not fail to be markedly influenced by daily contact with so alluring and stimulating a person'. Hugo Müller's shyness melted. He gratefully accepted an introduction by Warren into the scientific circles revolving round such figures as Martius, Peter Griess and Professor Hofmann, and like his patron later became President of the Royal Chemical Society.

Hugo Müller started as a research chemist in De La Rue. From the beginning he displayed the thoroughness typical of his countrymen. When an experiment called for palm leaves, it was not enough to obtain some from Kew; he also had a selection sent from Barbados, Calcutta and the Seychelles. He made it his business to know about all practical aspects of the firm's affairs, and Warren and Colonel Billy relied on him to run the fast expanding stamp department. When De La Rue changed from a partnership into a company he was persuaded to emerge from his laboratories and to become a director.

The de la Rues tried hard to make this studious man come out of his shell. His only hobby consisted of going on solitary botanical expeditions and bringing back specimens in his sponge-bag. Having despaired of ever luring him away from his bachelor existence, the family was delighted when at the age of forty-five he suddenly married Miss Elizabeth Crosby, the school friend of Warren's daughter Alice. He and his wife joined the de la Rue colony around Regent's Park, and moved into Park Square East. Two of Warren's children, his eldest son Warren William, and his daughter Alice and her husband, maintained stylish establishments in York Terrace.

Dr Müller's vital contribution was his part in perfecting 'fugitive inks', which in themselves provided enough security to satisfy the apprehensive Inland Revenue. In 1870 Ormond Hill wrote him a personal note: 'As regards the fugitiveness of the Postage Stamps, I think that in the absence of any evidence that the obliterating mark can be removed, we may rest satisfied that this is sufficient . . .' which for Board language amounted to praise.

*     *     *

Things were going so smoothly that Thomas could not resist rocking the boat a little; at least we can assume that it was Thomas, and not Warren, who was responsible for the sudden action brought by De La Rue against the stationery firm of John Dickinson & Co. in December 1856. Thomas had not had the opportunity to enjoy a meaty piece of litigation for some time, now. Admittedly, in this instance it was over the infringement of one of Warren's patents (for the envelope making machine) that the action was brought. But it is probable that Thomas spotted it first, Warren at that moment being heavily engaged in negotiations with The Board of Inland Revenue, and Colonel Billy with the production of the firm's first postage stamps. Their father was still active in the printing world. In 1853 he declared 'an improvement in the manufacture of paper', combining oxide of zinc with pulp, and in 1855 he brought out another patent for 'printing inks'. But in between he was quite possibly bored. His wife Jane was ailing. With time heavy on his hands Thomas, like an old war horse sniffing the air again, nudged Warren into the fray. Or so in the case against Dickinson it would appear, for Warren himself was on good terms with them and enjoyed Mr John Dickinson's hospitality.

Although De La Rue lost the action without their Counsel even being heard, Dickinson's delight was premature. They had reckoned without de la Rue tenacity. It was a rare experience for Thomas actually to *lose* a case and he was not going to let Dickinson get away with it. The Company rallied to the attack and re-opened proceedings. Miss Joan Evans shows us a record of the events in Fanny Dickinson's diary, which two months later included her dejected news of 'an adverse verdict on *every* point – and a most unjust one too . . . Poor dear Papa what a blow for him . . .' Fanny's cousin, Miss Phelps, noted that her uncle seemed not to mind about the money 'but he does care dreadfully about the imputation . . .' and the fact that 'de la Rue has been boasting about London that he has beat Dickinson . . . These hard envelope times'.

It is improbable that the 'boasting' de la Rue was any other than Thomas. Such behaviour was uncharacteristic of Warren or Colonel Billy. The matter was finally closed during the course of

May 25th and 26th, when the case of De La Rue v Dickinson was heard in the Court of Queen's Bench. There were four judges, two of whom, thought Fanny Dickinson, (who had taken up her position early on the first morning complete with a basket of stores to sustain her) 'were biased all thro' in De La Rue's favour'. The other two 'decided to leave before the case began'. As Fanny correctly surmised their remaining Lordships decided for De La Rue, and the firm received a financial settlement.

\* \* \*

In 1858 Jane de la Rue died from apoplexy, leaving a not overly devastated widower. Within a few months Thomas, then sixty-six, married Alice Marie, one of the three adventurous daughters of a Swedish gentleman called Carl André. The marriages of her two sisters landed them in Indianapolis and Vienna.

Alice Marie was young enough to have been Thomas's daughter. No de la Rues came to their wedding, which was performed in Stockholm with the British Consul for a witness. Although he had not yet retired from the Company, it is interesting to note that on this occasion Thomas did not mention that he was in 'trade'. All his life he had been content to be classified as a 'stationer', or 'cardmaker'. On his second marriage certificate he was styled simply 'gentleman'.

No one knows how Thomas came to meet Miss André. De La Rue had no business in Sweden. Thomas's, whatever it may have been, was of a private nature. Evidently he had some qualms about the swiftness of his remarriage, for he wrote to Warren shortly after it asking him 'not to publish anything' on the subject. But word of it leaked out. The damage was done when the rest of the family attended the wedding of Colonel Billy's brother-in-law, Dr Tanner. Until this moment the de la Rues had managed to keep it to themselves, but the effect of the Tanner nuptial festivities loosened their tongues. Spreading through the mid-Victorian gathering, the story was vicariously savoured in all its shocking aspects, including the circumstance of Thomas's 'new wife being a Roman Catholic'.

Three months after the wedding Thomas retired from the Company. He and his new wife divided their time between Westbourne Terrace, Hyde Park, and their country house at Sandy, Bedfordshire. Upon his retirement Thomas made some tough financial demands. He felt that but for him there would have been no Company of De La Rue. He asked for, and got, an annuity of £3,500, worth nearer thirty-five thousand today, plus a 5% interest on the £30,000 which he left in the business. He also transferred by deed £5,000 at 10% to the accounts of Warren and Colonel Billy. This was a steep rate of interest to charge one's own sons. At least Warren thought so. He felt equally strongly that were it not for his brother and himself, the de la Rue ship of state might have capsized.

'You have retired', Warren wrote to his father in September 1859, 'on terms which any disinterested person would pronounce liberal'. Reading between the lines there had been a fierce battle between father and sons about the terms of Thomas's retirement. Even with his children Thomas could not refrain from plunging into protracted argument. Warren was stung into the contemptuous understatement that 'in the arrangements which followed a lengthy discussion of terms, you fully and ably protected your own personal interests'.

After a crowded Scottish schedule, attending the British Association in Edinburgh and reading a paper on celestial photography at Aberdeen, Warren went off to the seclusion of the shooting lodges rented in Inverness by his American cousins-by-marriage, the Winans. There he had time to make an agonizing reappraisal of life with father. 'You allude to your separation from the business in Bunhill Row in terms not warranted by the facts', he declared to Thomas. 'For a number of years you enjoyed a large monopoly of shares in the business, namely four-ninths of the whole, the three other partners having five-ninths to divide amongst them. My share for a term was only one-ninth and at a period when I feel I was actively promoting the prosperity of the business and when that was by no means equivalent to my services; during the last term it was two-ninths and William's one-ninth, which at that period we would not have been contented with, with any other partner than a father . . .' Remembering that the period referred to covered the inception of De La Rue's postage stamp era, with all the work that it entailed for Warren and his brother, we cannot but think that they, not Thomas, had cause for grievance.

'It appears to me', concluded Warren heatedly, 'that if my children were in my place and I in yours that it would be a subject of pride on my part to feel that after many years of labour I could retire with such a munificent income and leave my children in such a prosperous business to which I was linked by name and feeling'. It is sad to record that the sun went down upon their wrath. The antagonism between father and sons never disappeared.

# CHAPTER VII

# *The builder's mates*

Throughout the hot summer of '57 Colonel Billy overhauled the administration of Bunhill Row. The business had been growing so fast that there had been no time in which to take stock. After ten booming years a trade recession was clouding the national scene, a factor which decided the de la Rue brothers that a thorough reassessment of output by men and machines was overdue. Week after week the foremen of each department were called in. As queries arose they in their turn sent for their men. The entire proceedings were taken down in shorthand and the result is as good as a play, dominated by Colonel Billy in his role of Chief Inquisitor, with the supporting cast consisting of Augustus Fry's son Fred, and Mr Tolmie, chief foreman, and character parts filled by miscellaneous old timers and artful dodgers.

From the outset Colonel Billy revealed that he had no illusions about the little tricks of factory life. It was no good, he said, for the foremen just to poke their heads round the doors in the mornings and ask if everybody was there, for 'of course they said they were'. And, he added, to confuse the issue 'they all rush down to the water closets about 8'. He understood that the heatwave was not conducive to work and that 'in this hot weather a man is much more inclined to sit down and drink cold water'. After gently chiding Miss Morrison, a book-keeper, for her want of system, he suggested it might be fun to send her account books to the British Museum. The foreman of Black Bordered Notepaper was rash enough to produce an undated bill. 'To what period does it refer since there has been a world?' he cried in exasperation. Quickly he worked out sums to show that production figures were not in fact as favourable as those submitted to him.

The old timers did not appreciate the cross questioning. 'I have been here since the reign of George the Fourth', said one, Brealey, defensively. 'You might have been here since the reign of Queen Ann', retorted Colonel Billy, 'and still your system might be bad'. To another, Solomon, he thundered accusingly: 'You don't do anything – you merely superintend'. Solomon protested that it was not his fault if a machine was idle, maintaining, in an impassioned cry from Labour to Management: 'It is for *you* to keep it alive. It is like a theatre. Till you get a certain amount in, it don't pay for the cost of opening the theatre'.

At one point the shorthand writer politely inserted in brackets: 'Wm de la Rue enjoys his joke'. And yet in spite of his sarcasm Colonel Billy tried hard to be fair. Although the foremen were the chief victims of his broadsides, he singled out a few for praise. It especially dismayed him to learn that if a dispute arose between men and overseers, the word of the latter was invariably law. He resolved that this injustice be avoided, urging each hand to take care to keep 'a proper account of his day's work' so that he might get the credit due to him.

In this spring cleaning of Bunhill Row no small corner was overlooked. As a result the foremen grasped that there was more to overseeing than checking men in and out, and the men could feel that under more efficient supervision their virtues, as well as their shortcomings, would be noted. The effects of Colonel Billy's efficiency drive were felt for the rest of the century. A boy employee, who joined the Company in late Victorian times observed: 'It had a tradition for being a comfortable firm with a happy atmosphere, most of the employees had been there a long time . . . the factories were clean and well maintained and the management was strict'. The de la Rue brothers could not have wished for better comment.

\*       \*       \*

It was early days for employers to bestir themselves about factory welfare. A journalist wrote approvingly in 1857: 'Solicitous to improve the condition of all in their employment, the Proprietors (of De La Rue) have latterly induced them to abandon the practice of taking beer twice during the hours of labour and in lieu have remitted half an hour from the general day's work. A marked social improvement has been the result'. To encourage their people to take tea rather than beer, Warren and Colonel Billy helped instigate a Tea Society. Its original purpose was to supply employees with 'tea for their evening meal at 5 o'clock daily and with tea and sugar to be taken home by them on Friday evenings'. Supplies were bought wholesale and sold at a low charge. Small profits accumulated, and the de la Rues suggested these be put to the credit of a provident fund for the benefit of the work people. Grants were made 'at death in case of deserving persons overtaken by misfortune'. A library was started 'for the use of all'. The Tea Society had grown out of a previous organization called 'The Men's Gift Fund', which started as early as 1842 and was considered enlightened because it did, in fact, bestow equal benefits for men and women.

The Press applauded these developments, calling them 'almost unique in industrial organizations', and recommending that they be 'taken as a model and exemplar of the good which may be accomplished by similar means in all establishments in which a large number of people are employed'.

The committee of foremen in Bunhill Row was induced to support two local hospitals, the Huguenot, and the Royal Chest Hospital in the City Road, thereby enabling its members to receive special treatment at these establishments. The de la Rue brothers set the lead by being governors of the

Huguenot, and financial supporters of the Royal Chest Hospital.

In other respects working conditions were still tough in Mid-Victorian De La Rue. Instead of latterday canteens and surgeries Bunhill Row had 'a few first aid boxes about', and there was the Bunhill Fields Coffee Tavern, where 'a good dinner could be got for 6d'. Some of the men brought their food to work and hotted it up in a dinner-warmer over the boilers. But these rigours were typical of the times. Despite them the de la Rue brothers established an *entente* with their work people which died hard; it did much to tide the firm over the dire misfortunes which were to be incurred by the successive members of their family.

CHAPTER VIII

# *The master builders:*
# *Warren and William Frederick de la Rue*

Although De La Rue gained a foothold in India by printing stamps
for the East India Company, it was Perkins Bacon who continued
to supply the Colonies with most of their stamps. Holding sway
over all negotiations were the Crown Agents. In 1858 a new
Agent General was appointed, one Penrose Julyan. The appointment of this man, with a name reminiscent of an Elizabethan
Cornishman, was a turning point for De La Rue.

Penrose Julyan was given to making sweeping gestures. By an
oversight Perkins Bacon, racing to meet the hugely increased
demand for penny and twopenny English stamps, did not consult
him before showing a new Colonial stamp to the Treasury. Deeply
insulted, he forced them to surrender to him their stamp dies and
plates for the Cape of Good Hope, Mauritius, Trinidad, Western
Australia, Ceylon, Saint Helena, the Bahamas, Natal and St Lucia.
He wondered to whom he should award them instead.

De La Rue had already executed a small Ceylonese order
promptly and efficiency. Mr Julyan was also impressed by the
firm's security record for the Inland Revenue. Moreover he discovered the man in charge of De La Rue's overseas printing to be
a man of action after his own heart: he and Colonel Billy took to
each other on sight. So well did they get on that they hardly ever
found it necessary to write anything down. When one or other of
his Colonial charges needed new stamps, from now onwards
Penrose Julyan simply handed the requirements over to Colonel

95

Billy, bestowing on him the courtesy title of 'Engraver to the Agents General for the Crown Colonies'.

It transpired that one of the Colonies, Mauritius, wanted paper currency as well. Although Perkins Bacon were already established as banknote printers and De La Rue had never ventured into this field, Penrose Julyan remained stoutly consistent. He refused to recommend the firm which had once snubbed him, and at the end of 1859 awarded De La Rue the small but auspicious contract to print Mauritian five pound, one pound and ten shilling notes. They were luxuriously produced by copperplate on paper from Turner's mill at Maidstone. Bound into books of 500, each with its own counterfoil, they resembled cheques. Every one was signed individually by the Treasurer. This was an extravagant method of making banknotes, but for De La Rue it was a start. (The Mauritian was the first of some 109 issues of banknotes to be made by the Company for various countries).

\*     \*     \*

As soon as a new country draws its first breath it needs its own postal and currency issues. Thus the firm came to be intimately associated with the birth of nations. The de la Rues tried to ensure that the Company had a representative in attendance whenever it was evident that another country was about to emerge. It was the same with deaths. Before a president or king was cold in his coffin, stamp essays must be ready depicting perfect heads of his heir. No sooner had King Leopold I of the Belgians died in 1865 than Warren initiated a correspondence concerning stamps for Leopold II. The brothers realised that business lay in being a step ahead of history.

When there was a prospect of a united Italy, Colonel Billy went hurrying off to Turin, its first capital. Pausing only to make occasional forays to Rome, in 1862 he settled down to lay siege to the Minister of Finance, Commander Sella. He sent round proposals 'for the production of postage and other stamps for the

homas de la Rue's first playing cards. *Top row* 1834, the pack that nearly ruined him: *middle row* 1840, his return to conventionality: *bottom row* 1832, his original pack

B. Travelling chess board designed by Peter Mark Roget, compiler of the *Thesaurus* exhibited by De La Rue at the Great Exhibition, 1851

De La Rue playing cards designed by Owen Jones for *left* Queen Victoria, *centre* Prince Albert, *right* The Prince of Wales

Kingdom of Italy for a contract of seven years', suggesting that the stamps should first be produced under the supervision of an Italian agent in Bunhill Row, and be of the same quality and size as those supplied by De La Rue for England.

The officials in Turin were pleased with the proposals. Three days later Colonel Billy sent a wire to Bunhill Row addressed to Thomas de la Rue, who had come out of retirement to hold the fort: 'Have order for Original Head Process proposal most likely accepted'. While awaiting a definite answer Colonel Billy employed his time in exploring other Italian fields. His telegram continued: 'Ultimately shall supply Italian railway tickets'.

Warren hastened to his brother's side to lend support. He wrote dutifully to his father at the first opportunity:
'My dear Sir,
I leave this evening for Milan. I shall proceed thence to Genoa direct; from Genoa to Leghorn by land, and thence by rail to Florence; this will occupy a week . . .' He describes how he has spent his time 'faisant l'antichambre', an experience to be undergone by many a future salesman, 'that is, I have been waiting the arrival of the Minister, then I have had to wait for an appointment . . .'

It was worth waiting – all the De La Rue proposals were accepted. Warren then spent some time in instructing a senior official, the Cavaliere Perazzi, how to make temporary stamps, and this move was also rewarding: 'Chevalier Perazzi has done wonders for us', he wrote, 'We must treat him with the greatest consideration because in all probability he will be sent to London'. With typical generosity he adds, 'William's point of the wedge has been pretty well driven home . . . it is to him that we owe the order'. Actually it was the combination of Warren's scientific knowledge and Colonel Billy's salesmanship which made the de la Rue brothers a formidable team in the field.

Accompanied by his wife Emma and daughter Ellen, Colonel

Billy made a return journey to Italy in December 1863. He explored the proposed premises for the Italian printing plant in 'the buildings and grounds of the Palais dei Martisi', and supervised the setting up of the establishment.

It all took a long time. Colonel Billy and his family were still detained in Turin in mid-January. Warren wrote encouragingly from London: 'If the cry is ultimately to be "Italy for the Italians" (i.e. should the Italian stamps be ultimately produced entirely in Turin and none in Bunhill Row) and Signor Mollino is inclined to stump up some ready in a handsome way, why . . . we could but sell ourselves to the "divil". I recollect James Nasmith's visit to Russia when he heard about the railroads. He went out to sell locomotives but finding our Americans (the Winans cousins) strongly in possession, instead of coming away sulkily he offered to sell them boiler plates, forgings, rivets or himself . . . And I recollect in one of Marryat's novels that a lady gained time when she fell into the pirates' hands by temporizing and did not lose her virtue'.

The advantage of being brothers in business was that they could be frank with each other without fear of being misconstrued. Thus Warren wrote to Colonel Billy again: 'Don't shut the door quite close against the foe; it may stop our chance of bleeding him . . .' Keeping 'the door open' exhausted Colonel Billy. He and his womenfolk went to Paris to recuperate. They joined their American cousins, did some shopping, and looked after the Cavaliere Perazzi, who was already en route from Turin to Bunhill Row to learn printing à la De La Rue. Warren was not swept off his feet by the victory in Italy. He sent his brother the level-headed comment: 'The contract I do not think will last over the first five years because by that time the Italian Authorities will . . . have become masters of our methods of printing . . . we must take care that we have a spanking good profit supposing we ever sink the plant we erect in Turin . . .' Then, in case he had been too dampening, he changed to a jollier note: 'Thanks for the venison. In the interim between the announcement of its arrival and your letter it had become rather elevated, so that I sent it to a friend who I hope appreciates it in prime condition. If not he can pass it on to another friend, and thus the single haunch may be the means of conferring favours on a great number of individuals'.

In April 1864 the de la Rues declined the Italian Government's request to 'manufacture postage or commercial stamps in Italy'. They felt that their 'numerous undertakings' in London prevented them from conducting a business 'in a distant country involving so many serious responsibilities . . .' a polite way of saying that neither brother could spare any further time on Italian visits. Instead they expressed willingness to help the Italians set up on their own, and to this end put their hearts into training the Cavaliere Perazzi. Falling at once into an easy camaraderie with him, Colonel Billy confided: 'My dear Cavaliere, Yesterday was the fête of St Derby and this time I managed to win a Five pound note . . .'

Delighted by this treatment a grateful Italy conferred the order of St Maurice and St Lazare on both brothers. In a letter to Baron Hambro, who was helping the Italians to establish their finances, Cavour referred to Colonel Billy as 'mon ami'.

# CHAPTER IX

## *Confederate castles in the air*
## *or the strange case of the* Bermuda

The most dramatic of De La Rue's current 'numerous under-takings' was the printing of stamps for the Confederates. By February 1861 the seven southerly 'Slave States', with Jefferson Davis as President, had formed themselves into the Confederate States of America; by April the war of Secessionist South against Federalist North had started; and by the end of the year Major B. F. Ficklin had arrived in England to head the Confederates' buying mission.

Although Ben Ficklin has been called the 'Mystery Man of the Confederacy', he wasted no time being mysterious with the de la Rues. Within a matter of days he moved in on them, and made Bunhill Row his headquarters. From there on February 11th he dispatched no less than eight telegrams, and sent out for twelve copies of Spense's *On the American Union*. On March 12th he requested De La Rue, through their Paris agents, to obtain for him: 'Twelve dozen First Class Quality Kid Skin Gloves' in sizes varying from $6\frac{1}{4}$ to $6\frac{3}{4}$ in different colours and '3 dozen similar pairs all in white'. What B. F. Ficklin wanted with 180 assorted pairs of ladies' gloves we shall never know. De La Rue made no comment, but took care to charge them to the Major's account, both in francs and pounds.

On March 18th he asked for a loan. The firm lent him £1,000 in cash, and three days later another £1,238 7s 1d. At this time the capital of De La Rue was £73,000, so that the amount of ready cash could not have been more than £10,000. The loans were therefore comparatively large. De La Rue also paid the men recruited by the Confederacy in Scotland, who were to travel to America to manufacture its stamps with De La Rue equipment.

At the outset of the American Civil War British sympathy was fairly equally divided between both sides. Later in the war Queen Victoria declared the Federalists to be 'such ruffians', and the bulk of upper class and industrial England, especially the cotton magnates, agreed with her. But Colonel Billy was ready to assist the Confederates from the outset. One wonders why.

The answer must have lain in personal relationships. Colonel Billy was especially close to the Winans's; he and his family had just returned from travelling with these American cousins in Europe. He had undoubtedly enjoyed their hospitality in America on his 1850 visit. They were not only leading Confederates, they were also excessively wealthy as a result of their railroads. Had Ben Ficklin failed to honour his bills the Winans's could have covered them many times over. There is every reason to suppose that it was at their instigation that Colonel Billy agreed to so immediate an involvement.

At the time Warren was abroad again. Colonel Billy wrote from Bunhill Row to give him a picture of the home front. Major Ficklin, he said, was dominating the scene and taking up most of his time. But still, the Major was paying his debts. He 'gave us a cheque for 5000 £ . . . I have paid away for him about £2,500 but he will give me another 2000 £ in a day or so'. The Company would make a profit on the Confederate order, in itself worth nearly £5,000. With a light heart Colonel Billy went up to Glasgow to see Ficklin off.

\*　　　\*　　　\*

The postage stamps which the Confederates had ordered from De La Rue were the Five Cents Blue or 'the London Print', as philatelists call it, with its head of Jefferson Davis, and the Orange

One Cent, with the head of John C. Calhoun. Both were designed by Joubert de la Ferté. The Five Cents Blue has the distinction of being the only American stamp ever to be printed abroad and remain current for any considerable time. The Orange One Cent was destined never to be current at all.

In November 1862 Colonel Billy mentioned dispatching 'a very large quantity of goods all the American order of Ficklin . . .' This included the first shipment of five million Blue Five Cents. Due to the seamanship of Captain John Wilkinson, a hero of the Confederate Navy, these stamps were safely delivered aboard the blockade runner *Robert E. Lee* to Wilmington, North Carolina.

The following March another blockade runner, the ill-fated *Bermuda*, left Liverpool. The passenger list included the Scottish printers hired by De La Rue, and the cargo represented the fruits of Ficklin's De La Rue-aided shopping expeditions. It contained tea, coffee, drugs, surgical instruments, saddlery and cutlery bearing such legends as:

JEFF. DAVIS

OUR FIRST PRESIDENT

The Right Man in the Right Place

Stowed away in the hold were some tympan boxes from Bunhill Row. Inside them were the rest of the five million Blue Five Cents and the first Orange One Cents.

The ship arrived in St George's, Bermuda, and lay up there for five weeks. While venturing in the direction of Charleston on April 27th 1863, she was captured by the Federalist ship *Mercedita*. She was taken to Philadelphia, adjudged a legal prize by the Federal Court, and sold with all her contraband cargo – all, that is, except for the stamps from De La Rue. According to an order from the Attorney General, these were ordered to be reduced to pulp.

Among the Reports of Cases Argued and Adjudged in the Supreme Courts of the U.S. in December 1865, is one on the

*Bermuda* case. It throws another light on the story: 'At the time of the capture and after the boat was boarded, the captain's brother by his order threw overboard two small boxes and a package which he swore contained postage stamps . . .'

'On the vessel', continues the Report, 'were several persons called in various letters "government passengers" being in fact "artists" from Scotland. One of them carried a letter written from a Mr C. Straker of the Stationery department, 80 Bishopsgate Within, 26 Leadenhall St. London . . .' This letter, addressed to the Confederate Government by the aggrieved Mr Straker, complained of a Confederate Commissioner (Major Ficklin) who 'served me very shabbily and ungentlemanlike. I had many interviews with him and gave him all necessary information; furnished him with a list of requirements, compromising myself with several workmen and put myself to many inconveniences. He admitted my price being proper and correct and led me to believe that he would give me his order, but *having got out of me all that he could* he then entrusted the order with another house' (De La Rue). There is something curiously affecting about Mr Straker's impotent cry addressed to the leaders of a lost cause, concerning a stamp issue which came to be known philatelically as 'The Lost Shipment', in a letter which lost its way and was never delivered.

Mr Straker might have felt better had he known there was one bill for which the crafty Ficklin did not pay Colonel Billy. In addition to the stamps seized on the *Bermuda* there was also a small matter of a 'Super Royal Printing Press in satin-lined Tympan Box with Six Inking Rollers'. For these the Confederate States owed De La Rue £294 8s 4d ever after.

# CHAPTER X

## *With their own hands*

Vital to the growth of Thomas's house were the long term 'print-ing contracts initiated by his sons. The Company was to print all postage stamps for India for 71 years, for Ceylon for 73 years, for Great Britain for 55 years . . . and the foreign order books show that other lasting associations were started with the Governments of Italy, Portugal, Uruguay and Ecuador.

The de la Rues made their own printing improvements as they went along. The choice of stamp colours for instance, was still limited – Thomas set to and patented two-colour processes. Work needed to be done on watermarks – Colonel Billy did it. Improve-ments to paper were necessary – Warren and Dr Müller busied themselves with printers' rags. The value of their homework was soon to be seen, and to keep pace with production they urgently needed more space. They rented all the neighbouring houses in Bunhill Row, bought two freeholds in Blue Anchor Alley, established offices in Liverpool and Paris, but were forced to close down their New York branch in September 1861, when they lost £100 on 'Sale of Mr P. Supple's furniture etc on his leaving New York in consequence of the Civil War'.

The old stationery business supported the new security printing projects. A surprisingly good seller was the Improved Indelible Diary. Apparently compiled for the exclusive benefit of Warren and Colonel Billy, its sales showed their interests to have been shared by numbers of other prosperous mid-Victorian males. It contained such varied pieces of information as the 'Precise Details of the Occultations Visible at Greenwich', when there would be no real night at Edinburgh, the birthdays of Galileo, the Royal Society and Jenny Lind, the day when dividends fell due on India bonds, and the seasons for every conceivable form of game shooting. There was a reverent preoccupation with Royal deaths and a morbid interest in earthquakes, revolutions, fires and other assorted calamities. On May 15th it was felt essential to commemorate that the Manor of Manchester was sold for £3,000 in 1579. The diminutive Indelible Diary reflected in miniature the strange tastes and the times of the brothers de la Rue.

In November 1862 Colonel Billy was able to report that notepaper work was expanding steadily. The Commissioner of the Rajah of Mysore alone had just ordered '5,000 reams of f.cap paper with watermark . . . Moreover he says he requires annually from £1,500 to £2,000 of ordinary stationery for the public offices . . .' Referring to Bunhill Row as 'this immense establishment' the *Art Journal* described the different kinds of notepaper produced there, including 'all the chaste varieties of wedding Stationery'.

Between 1857 and 1866 De La Rue output of railway tickets doubled, and the packs of playing cards sold rose from 93,060 in 1856 to 265,048 in 1868. Thomas could survey his enlarged house with pride. Although he would not have admitted as much to his sons, he knew very well that it was in good hands. Otherwise he would never have dreamt of leaving his money in it.

# CHAPTER XI

## *Death in the house*

From the day of his wedding to the Swedish girl Alice Marie, Thomas de la Rue ceased to figure in the Company's affairs. His name does not reappear in any of its correspondence. During the summer of 1866, when he was in his seventy-fourth year, he went suddenly to pieces. He took to his bed in his London house, and it was all over in a matter of three weeks, his death certificate listing the cause as 'break-up of constitution'. Although he had been fully retired from business for six years, his occupation was recorded as 'Wholesale Stationer'. Technically, at least, Thomas died as he had live nearly all his life – in 'trade'.

Alice Marie followed the precedent set by Thomas. He had married her a year after Jane's death. She remarried within a year of his. She became the wife of Sir Richard Temple Rennie, a successful barrister whose father was a one time Governor of the Falkland Islands. Having acquired this grander background she faded quietly into it, and did not cross the de la Rue path again.

It had never occurred to Thomas to bother about his parents' graves. A distant relation wrote from St Peter Port to Warren to say that her husband had recently come across the tombstone of Eleazar and Rachel de la Rue in a 'stone-dresser's yard', where it had been lying unpaid for and unclaimed 'for over 40 years'. Warren, on the other hand, had a strong sense of family duty. However deep the conflict between father and son had been, when it came to making the arrangements for Thomas's burial Warren saw to it that his father's remains were placed in the currently fashionable cemetery of Kensal Green, and he bought the surrounding space for de la Rue descendants with the request that he himself should be buried beside his father. In this respect the image of Thomas as *pater familias* was dutifully preserved.

Thomas's will was an impersonal document covering barely half a page. He did not make a single bequest concerning a personal possession. There was not one word of appreciation for a retainer in his household, or worker in his firm. It is true that by the time of his death his two elder sons did not stand in need of material assistance. Yet considering how much Warren and Colonel Billy had helped with the building of Thomas's house, a word of acknowledgement would not have come amiss. By contrast to their wills, which were to be crowded with affectionate references to friends, relations and employees, his was a lonely affair. After a £1,000 had been put at the immediate disposal of Alice Marie the rest of his £39,000 was divided equally between her and the five children of his marriage with Jane. He made one final dig at Warren and Colonel Billy to the effect that 'each of my sons shall give credit . . . on account of the share thereby given to him of the money which I gave and advanced to him upon the dissolution of my partnership in the year 1859 but without being charged with any interest thereon'. That was all.

After Thomas's death a more relaxed atmosphere prevailed in Bunhill Row. Warren and Colonel Billy felt at liberty to widen their horizons. Warren became the guiding light of a scientific City body called 'The London Institution'. He and Dr Müller continued their electrical experiments, and devised 'their well known chloride of silver non-polarisable voltaic element of constant E.M.F. . . .' The Chemical Society commented that 'this piece of work was an exemplar of the two men, showing the grace of the one (Warren) and the deftness of the other' (Müller).

By the year of the Vienna International Exhibition Hugo Müller had come to be regarded as an authority in his own right, and was invited to provide the chemical section of the Viennese report. If he was the prototype of the modern industrial chemist, Warren was something even rarer, 'an active promoter of an interest in science among his fellow Managers'. Now that it was possible to entrust Bunhill Row's laboratories wholly to Müller, and the running of the Company to Colonel Billy, he became President of the Royal Chemical Society. At the same time, as the Royal Astronomical Society recalled appreciatively, he was always ready to assist astronomical researches with his money and influence. When his eyesight started to fail he relinquished his connections with the daily solar photographic operations at Kew, for which he had devised 'entirely by himself' a telescope known as a 'photoheliograph'. His own reflecting telescope was eagerly accepted by Oxford University, who put up special buildings to house it.

Colonel Billy, confident that he had taken every care to protect the Company's present and future prosperity, began to take an interest in other businesses. He was nominated a director of the National Mercantile Assurance Society, which was in the process of amalgamating with the Eagle Star Insurance Company, and he became a director of Eagle Star itself. The satisfaction he gave to the Eagle Star board was indicated by the speed with which he was appointed first its deputy chairman, and then its chairman, within the space of three years.

His career was cut pathetically short. When only forty-six he developed cancer of the liver. He suffered for some months, but until the very end insisted upon trying to fulfil his commitments. Eagle Star minutes refer to his regular attendance at board meetings 'so long as his health permitted'. At the time of his death in August 1870 he was Chairman of Eagle Star, Senior Partner of De La Rue, and, as Engraver to the Crown Agents, was still responsible for advising on all Colonial security printing matters.

During his last year he expended precious energy upon

Tasmania's stamp problems. His illness clouded his judgement a little and he made a rare mistake by failing to take into account the size of the new De La Rue Tasmanian stamps. Being narrower and shorter than the old ones these did not fit the watermark on the existing paper, which the Tasmanian Government wanted to use up; yet Colonel Billy went on record as saying that the new stamps 'would fall in very well with the watermark'. After his death, unhappily, the Tasmanians called for an explanation, and the Company had to admit 'it would not have been possible to make surface printing plates to fit the paper in stock without involving an expense far beyond the paper itself. This however ought to have been pointed out by our late Mr W. F. de la Rue'.

Either Colonel Billy concealed from his brother the nature of his illness, or he himself did not realize its seriousness; otherwise it is impossible to understand how Warren could retire to enjoy the pursuit of his scientific studies only months before his beloved brother's cancer took its toll. Had he known the extent of Colonel Billy's ill health he would have insisted on resuming the task of running De La Rue himself. From the frequent codicils he added to his will in the final months of his life it would seem that Colonel Billy was in fact aware of his approaching death. He added the last one just three weeks before he died, requesting that his wife's relation, Emma Tanner, who had made her home with them in Harley Street, be allowed to keep all the furniture in her room there.

Although he left £60,000 he asked that his funeral should be 'plain and inexpensive'. Warren, heart-broken, did what was possible to comfort Colonel Billy's widow and children. He did not persuade the eldest child, Thomas, into the Company; allowing the boy to follow in his father's military as opposed to business, footsteps he personally supervised young Thomas's progress through Sandhurst.

# CHAPTER XII

## *Good house-keeping*

The passing of Colonel Billy left the firm in a state of upheaval. Warren's eldest son, Warren William, wrote dejectedly to Ormond Hill about 'the unsettled state in which we have been for the past few months in consequence of the illness of my poor Uncle'. However, there was so much work in hand in Bunhill Row that there was no alternative but to try to return to business as usual. Warren pulled himself together, put his scientific interests aside, and at the age of fifty-seven came out of retirement to lead the firm again as senior partner.

The only other partner was Jonah Nathan, who was soon due to retire. Warren's immediate task was therefore to augment the partnership. He thought himself fortunate in having two suitable candidates close at hand. He was able to call not only upon Warren William, his eldest, but also Thomas Andros, his second son, to support him as partners in Bunhill Row.

De la Rue fathers seem to have had an instinct for educating their sons in a manner well suited to the boys' capabilities. Warren William was a strange, if not eccentric person. Warren had him educated by tutors at home. Thomas Andros, comparatively extrovert, was given a more conventional upbringing at Rugby and Cambridge. Both boys followed the family tradition of entering De La Rue as soon as their studies were completed.

Warren was particularly delighted with the progress of his eldest son. When Warren William was only twenty-three, and had been with the firm a mere four years, 'he had developed so rapidly that he was able to take over his Uncle's work entirely'. In spite of his youth it was he who was now appointed to the position of Engraver to the Crown Agents, previously held by Colonel Billy. He inherited much of the latter's interest in business efficiency, and was for ever devising better methods of organization. If his communications lacked the grace of his father's or the force of Colonel Billy's his strength lay in a persistent refusal to take 'no' for an answer. He wore down his men by sheer weight of verbiage. Warren William was a slogger.

His attention to detail amounted almost to a fetish. He had been in Colonel Billy's shoes one month when he was already worrying about the firm's methods of recording Colonial transactions. In October 1870 he requested permission from Crown Agent Sir William Sargeant to make and keep a perfect record of all the Crown Colonies Stamp printing plates 'with an impression of each form printed on its own paper and in the proper colour'. It disturbed his tidy mind not to be able to make an instant reference to these without 'inconvenience and loss of time'. Sir William demurred, Warren William persisted, and by the end of November the required Colonial specimens lay neatly pigeon-holed in Bunhill Row.

That the coming era was a golden age for the firm was partly due to the meticulousness with which Warren William kept the customers satisfied. A series of correspondence with the Board of Inland Revenue demonstrates the extent of his conscientiousness. He was distressed because the firm appeared to have lost a single sheet of unprinted, unwatermarked paper. At once he informed the Board of the loss. He received no reply, either because the Board forgot to make one, or because it reckoned the matter to be so unimportant that none was necessary. Warren William thought otherwise. With something of his grandfather's terrier-like tenacity, and a patience which was a great deal more monumental than Thomas's, he burrowed away at the Board. 'Understanding that our letter of the 13th ulto of which we enclose a copy has been mislaid', he begins again, and one can almost hear the recipient in the Inland Revenue office stifling a yawn. Yet feeling it incumbent upon him to disclose every domestic detail about the missing piece of paper, Warren William persevered; 'the sheet was inadvertently separated from the ream to which it belonged by the Forewoman of the Gumming Department. As soon as she discovered her mistake she followed the man who was removing the work from her room and handed him the sheet done up in a roll of Crown paper. The man being in a hurry placed the sheet in the passage and unfortunately forgot to look for it until some hours afterwards, when he failed to find it. We believe that the roll must have been swept away and got into the general waste of our factory, and thus been destroyed'.

The Board could not but accept this earnest explanation of a misdemeanour so trivial that it would probably have passed unnoticed had attention not been drawn to it. Even if such precision appeared faintly ridiculous, the customers were impressed by the standards of efficiency upon which Warren William insisted throughout Bunhill Row.

*       *       *

De La Rue 'quality' stationery was maintaining its prestige, the copyright notepaper 'Imperial Treasury' and the 'Fine Old Turkey Mill' being 'in great demand in better class shops' in London, Paris and Rome. A pneumatic finish to facilitate handling and dealing improved the latest playing cards. The surface of the cards was slightly grooved by being rolled on prepared plates, so that there were little pockets of air between each card, which prevented them sticking together. This idea was contributed by the newest comer to the partnership, William Thomas Shaw 'a man of diplomatic charm', an old employee and de la Rue friend. Amid a spate of De La Rue patents, yet another member of the family,

THE BEST WISHES OF THE SEASON TO YOU.

C. Victorian greetings cards made by De La Rue, 1870

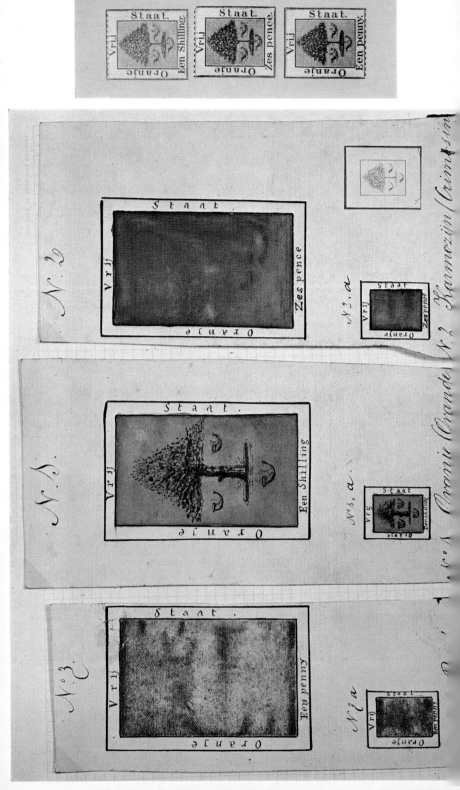

Warren's third son, Ernest, contributed ideas for firelighters, pocket books and bookmarkers.

De La Rue was now well enough known to be a target for caricature. *Punch* took aim at the firm's new greetings cards upon which unseasonable flowers bloomed at Christmas time, together 'with all manner of birds, beasts, actual and antediluvian, with gnomes and elves and nixies and pixies and even with little Watteau-ish men and maidens in the most charming costumes'. Fastidious Thomas might well have turned in his grave at such a lapse in De La Rue taste; he would have deplored the nixies and pixies however well they were selling, and concentrated, perhaps, on the Watteau-ish men and maidens as being the least abhorrent of these evils.

De La Rue diaries, packed with information about comets and eclipses, came in for the same kind of treatment by *Punch;*

> 'Oh how gladly you will prize
> Diaries from De La Rue
> Every sort and every size
> Oh how gladly you will prize!
> All the lore that in them lies –
> Mighty useful t'is to you . . .'

About this time the de la Rues attempted some book publishing, bringing out such relatively daring works as *Strange Stories from a Chinese Studio,* and *An Art Student in Munich* by the author of *The Vulture Maiden.* But on the whole they thought it safer to stick to books on backgammon and whist, which had the advantage of boosting their own products.

\*     \*     \*

Warren de la Rue's career was working up to a grand finale. By the time he came to retire in 1880 both the scientific and business aspects of his life were at their peak. A learned committee in Paris was compiling a fifteen-page dossier about him for the Académie des Sciences, to which he was an aspiring candidate.

The French did not underestimate him. 'La carrière de M. Warren de la Rue', they decided, 'est une des plus rémarquables qu'en puisse offrir comme exemple d'activité humaine . . .' Nor did they minimise the importance of the Company. They declared Warren to be the head of a house with 'un nom Européan et qui fait d'immenses affaires'. They enumerated his achievements, ranging from perfecting cochineal colouring to pioneering celestial photography. Astronomers all over the world, they said, should applaud his intelligence and perseverence. 'Une vie scientifique, si active et si fructueuse associée aux devoirs toujours remplis d'un grand industriel, donne un mérite tout particulier à celui qui a su deployer une si noble activité' . . . After this eulogy it is hardly necessary to add that Warren was unanimously elected to the Académie des Sciences.

Like national hopes for Britannia the 'immenses affaires' of De La Rue were destined to become mightier yet. Abroad the Company was winning more and more customers for postage stamps. At home, though, Perkins Bacon still printed all stamp denominations, including the One Penny. The *Globe* was the first publication to air the winter of discontent which was about to descend on De La Rue's rival. On March 7th 1877 a *Globe* correspondent mercilessly dissected Perkins Bacon's One Penny, the stamp for which there was the greatest public demand. He found nothing good to say about it; its paper was 'inferior to that of any other kind', its colouring material was soft and dusty 'which renders the use of any considerable number anything but pleasant', and it did not stick well because it was too thick and stiff. Its only merit to the Post Office ('a department of the Public Service regulated with so delicate an appreciation of small savings') was, remarked the *Globe* snidely, its liability to come off in letter boxes. Its 'notoriously unsatisfactory character' was apparent when compared with the receipt stamp. 'Everyone who has had the satisfaction of using a receipt stamp must be well aware of the superior character of this stamp over the other'.

At any time this would have been music in the ears of the receipt stamp's manufacturers, Thomas De La Rue and Sons. Now, when the Perkins Bacon contract was just about to expire, it was heavenly harmony. For the company in Bunhill Row the *Globe* article could not have been more opportune. It sowed the seeds of public dissatisfaction with Perkins Bacon at just the right moment, so that they were growing nicely by the time the Government invited seven firms including Perkins, Bradbury, Waterlow and De La Rue to tender for a One Penny order.

This was the firm's moment, its chance to establish its superiority over all-comers. It rose to the occasion with towering confidence. No tender can ever have been more comprehensive than the one it now submitted. It implied that by comparison with its own professionalism, Perkins Bacon were charming amateurs. Almost all 'the great States of Europe', it declared, had sought assistance from De La Rue, and the number of stamps the firm had supplied to India and the Colonies ran into 'billions', without a single complaint of forgery. It took the opportunity to extol the superiority of its letterpress method of printing (which it had done so much to develop) over the copper plate method of Perkins Bacon.

Surveying the scene from Olympian heights De La Rue thought, furthermore, that it was beneath them to descend into the arena and be ranked in consideration 'with other firms', mere mortals, who lacked their prodigious experience, practical skill, scientific knowledge and devotion to the work in hand 'in the shape of close personal supervision'. This supervision by the de la Rue family, and by Dr Hugo Müller, was their trump card. The Board of Inland Revenue was aware that the men at Bunhill Row were the acknowledged experts on their subject.

Among the Niagara of verbiage laboriously prepared for the

tender by Warren William, one light touch of Warren's is apparent, a thumbnail sketch of 'the skilled ... numberless Oriental craftsmen, who unfortunately combine with many of the subordinate officials in regarding the defraudment of the Revenue not only as a source of profit but as positively meritorious . . . ' For the rest, the firm's arguments were of a weighty order. Philatelists agree that the Board of Inland Revenue 'would have been crazy to have looked at anyone else'. De La Rue won the contract for the Penny Stamp.

When the news of their latest success arrived at Bunhill Row on June 27th 1879 it was received with equanimity. Three days later the Company briefly acknowledged the Board's acceptance of its tender, adding only the polite formality: 'be good enough to convey to your Board our best thanks for the additional mark of their confidence'. Considering that every postage stamp in Britain was shortly to be produced from Bunhill Row, this sounded like a complacent reaction, so certain had the de la Rues been of victory.

But there was nothing complacent about the series of experiments upon which they now embarked in the Bunhill Row laboratories to perfect their printing of the 'Penny'. They worked on them for the rest of the summer. The red colour which the Company proposed to use had a copper base. To ensure it was harmless three leading toxicologists were called in, Doctors Dupré and Murrell of the Westminster Hospital's School of Medicine, and Dr Ringer, Professor of Medicine at University College. Pursuing their experiments 'with the utmost vigour' the doctors 'administered the colouring matter *without any* effect whatever in large and repeated doses to various lower animals as well as to man'. The Company undertook these researches voluntarily. Indeed until reports were submitted to the Board of Inland Revenue, the latter was unaware that any such work had been carried out. Much impressed the Board agreed to the proposed 'Copper red', and noted that the Company's monopoly of stamp printing had not gone to its head. So far from relaxing their efforts De La Rue had redoubled them.

The quantities of stamps involved were to be astronomical. De La Rue day books record that from November 1879 to June 30th 1881, 1,462,584,000 One Penny stamps alone were delivered. The housing of production on this scale created a new problem. Already committed to India's entire postal needs, as well as to Colonial ones, all Great Britain's in addition now entailed a major expansion. To its existing cluster of Bunhill Row factories the Company added the Crown and the George Works. The showpiece was the new Star Works, 'which we may say', wrote De La Rue to the Board of Inland Revenue, 'stands unrivalled in the nature of the accommodation it affords'.

It was especially constructed for stamp work, each floor consisting of one large room 'for the proper purpose of supervision'. Heavy machinery could be placed anywhere, 'even on the top floor'. Work for the British Inland Revenue now occupied five factories, an 'immense' area as the firm pointed out. If these British orders were not maintained, the Company would have many idle square feet. De La Rue tried to lure the Board of Inland Revenue into making a long term contract, emphasizing the economic benefits which would accrue to all concerned. The Board was reluctant to agree; perhaps it was beginning to fear a De La Rue domination. At any rate it would only commit itself to extending the one penny contract from seven to ten years. But the partnership could not grumble; if it fulfilled all its British contracts as satisfactorily as its Colonial ones, it had little to fear. No printing house could have asked for a rosier future.

# CHAPTER XIII

# *Household gods*

The winter after Warren's retirement his sons and daughters spent some anxious weeks at his house in Portland Place, trying to support their father through a severe attack of pneumonia and to encourage their distressed mother, who was alternating between bouts of hope and despair. As well as supervising his nursing the fragile-looking Georgiana also coped bravely with Warren's voluminous and cosmopolitan correspondence. Many of her replies to his well wishers were written in impeccable French. 'Il est faible comme un enfant', she grieved at the end of one to a Parisian scientist. While he was still critically ill, word came from Paris to say that he was to be made a Commandant of the Légion d'Honneur. This recognition by the country of his upbringing gave him considerable comfort. Georgiana wrote to say so, and to accept the honour on his behalf.

At length he responded to the various treatments and to the care of his devoted family. His long illness revealed, incidentally, that Warren had nothing of the reserve associated with stern and distant Victorian father figures. Georgiana's thank-you letters emphasize that their children stayed at Warren's side not so much out of filial duty, as out of their deep affection for him.

Once he was on the way to recovery Warren William and Thomas Andros returned their attentions to Bunhill Row, which was then abustle with the first postal orders for the G.P.O., and with a new invention, the 'anti-stylographic nibbed pen'. As the first practical fountain pen it was a piece of evolution in the stationery field. A self-feeding reservoir pen with an ordinary nib, it could write 'continuously'. Further developments resulted in 'The Swift reservoir penholder', reported by the *Stationery Trade Journal* to be 'one of the greatest successes of the day . . . The ink can be regulated in its flow to suit all hands and when not in use is effectively shut off at the very point of the pen . . .' One would have thought it difficult to improve on such a marvel but the 'Pelican' pen managed to do so, sporting an 'improved gold nib' and larger ink capacity. The 'Swift's' memory was perpetuated in the badge of the De La Rue Cricket Club which consisted of a garter, similar to the watermark in the early stamps 'enclosing a swift in flight against a background of stumps and bails'.

*　　*　　*

Warren did not resume an active part in business affairs. After his illness he left the running of the firm to his sons. Once more De La Rue was ruled by a partnership of de la Rue brothers. Warren William and Thomas Andros had married within a year of each other. The elder brother's childless marriage to Miss Helen Norton was not a success. Seven years later they were divorced. Thomas Andros's marriage to Miss Emily Speed, on the other hand, was a partnership which lent lasting distinction to the London scene. His father-in-law was a successful advocate known as 'Railway' Speed, who benefited from the property disputes left by the steam engine in its wake across England. With wealthy parents on either side Thomas Andros and Emily were well endowed. They were the first de la Rues to cherish social ambitions and be interested in living really grandly. Their country cousins dreaded having them to stay for fear they would be bored while away from the glitter of London, where they were building a house in Cadogan Square.

Not without some of the eccentricity which marked the character of his brother, Thomas Andros insisted on the other houses in the Square being renumbered so that his could be fifty-two, the

119

same number as the amount of playing cards in a pack. Doubtless the neighbours were placated by gifts of De La Rue notepaper bearing their new addresses, but they soon discovered that they had other cause to regret the arrival of Thomas Andros. He was one of the most enthusiastic party givers in the West End. Although his house was so constructed as to be detached from the adjacent ones by a few inches, it is improbable that so small a separation safeguarded his neighbours' sleep. The de la Rue parties were large and late.

Warren William had sporting tastes like his Uncle Billy, but on a loftier scale. Maintaining a large establishment at Newmarket, he devoted his leisure to racing with such seriousness that when his horse Trayles subsequently won the Ascot Gold Cup, the Alexandra Plate and the Goodwood Cup in one year, he named a house after him and erected twin models of Trayles's head over the gateposts. The single-mindedness with which Warren William pursued the sport of kings cost him not only his wife, but a small fortune. He reverted to a rather splendid bachelor existence which he divided between Newmarket and his house in York Terrace, Regent's Park, where a special lift was built for the purpose of sending down his false teeth to be cleaned by his valet.

Excessive single-mindedness and a sense of humour combine infrequently together. Warren William had no sense of humour whatsoever. On the occasions when his father, or his uncle, would have parried a business thrust with a quick retort and an amused shrug, he remained like his Sovereign, unamused. Rival Jacob Perkins wrote banteringly to the Lieutenant Governor of St Vincent that 'there are many ladies who practise wood engraving who could produce a tolerable imitation of De La Rue stamps'. Devoid of repartee, Warren William could not think of an answer other than to quote back Perkins Bacon's innuendo in full, with the comment: 'it can only have been prompted by trade jealousy'.

In April 1897 something extraordinary happened. An actual complaint against De La Rue stamps was received from Lagos. In the ensuing events Warren William proved that his lack of verbal rapier-play was a deficiency of relative unimportance compared with his capacity for withstanding a long bombardment. The Lagos complaint was followed by thirteen more from other Colonies – sixteen to be precise, pointed out Warren William, unabashed, since Cyprus, the Bahamas and the Straits Settlements made two complaints each. Every one found fault with De La Rue gumming. After the first few grumbles a lesser man, or one with a thinner skin, might well have become alarmed. Warren William, on the contrary, settled down systematically to break up the complaints into categories as follows: the disputed stamps were either (a) tested by De La Rue and their gumming found to be satisfactory or (b) not tested because the Colonies in question neglected to send them back for analysis (thereby putting themselves in an inferior position straight off) or (c) as in the case of Tobago, Grenada and the Bahamas, tested and their gum found to have deteriorated through exposure to moisture.

When yet another complaint arrived, this time from Zululand, no less a body than the British Board of Inland Revenue sprang to defend De La Rue from Colonial attack. Having examined the stamps the Board exonerated the Company, and criticised the Crown Agents for not ensuring that unused sheets were kept in receptacles properly suited to tropical conditions. After the oracle had thus spoken any further Colonial gumming complaints would have fallen on stony ground. No more were made.

\*     \*     \*

In March 1888 the realization dawned on the British public that it was nourishing a stamp making monopoly in its midst. The House of Commons reverberated with attacks upon the conduct of the Board of Inland Revenue. The Member for Prestwich, Lancashire, demanded to know why the Board had awarded De La

Rue the consolidated contract for all British stamps some eight years ago, when other competitors had offered lower prices. Words like 'favouritism' and 'extravagance' filled the air. The newspapers took up the cry.

The Chancellor of the Exchequer, Mr Goschen, replied soothingly that 'owing to the fall in prices and improved processes of production it is tolerably certain that when the contract expires in 1890, considerable savings will be effected'. This proved to be wishful thinking on his part. For the next twenty years the stamps continued to be printed by De La Rue at the same prices – thanks to the barrage now set up by Warren William. It took no genius to perceive that this was an untimely moment for the Company to be caught in the spotlight of a national controversy, and that immediate onslaught must be made upon De La Rue's detractors, notably the Member for Prestwich, Lancashire.

Warren William attacked this gentleman, Mr Mowbray, accordingly: 'The statement which you addressed to the House of Commons last Monday, with reference to certain of our Government Printing Contracts, having received new prominence from its republication in a distorted and still more injurious form in yesterday's *Daily News*, we deem it necessary to address you on the subject'. After this reasonably polite opening, he went on to suggest that the Member had not the slightest idea of what he was talking about. To declaim upon so specialised a subject as stamp printing a specialised knowledge was necessary, and that the Member clearly did not have. Was Mr Mowbray even aware that in the London School Board printing contracts there was a difference between the highest and lowest tenders of 57 per cent?

How dare the ill-informed Member presume to damage the firm's good name in its 'general business at home and foreign business . . .' on the eve of its Government Contract's renewal?

Mr Mowbray was silenced, and a Government Inquiry subsequently accepted the firm's evidence completely. The niggling question which remained in the public mind, nevertheless, was the same as Queen Victoria's after Mad King Ludwig of Bavaria committed suicide in a lake with his doctor: 'Surely the whole thing must have been very badly managed?' The episode, though closed, was not forgotten.

\*     \*     \*

Living long enough to see the clouds of immediate controversy pass over, Warren senior died in 1889. As was to be expected there was a chorus of eulogies in learned journals. Leaving these aside we might pause for a moment over his will, which in his case was an intimate testament of his affections. He listed his appreciation of everyone who had helped him beginning, as Thomas never brought himself to do, with the members of his own family. He spoke of his 'dear wife Georgiana', and his son Warren William' for whom I have the greatest affection and who has done so much to ensure my prosperity', but since he was already 'very wealthy' he did not leave him anything except a 'token' gift of £15,000. As with Warren's long-ago school reports there was one touch which removed any odour of sanctimoniousness. Perhaps his coachman George Emmans had recently committed a driving offence which jarred his otherwise equable master, for when distributing his fortune of £350,000 Warren remembered in a codicil to revoke the £200 legacy to the aforesaid. For the rest, as a panorama of late Victorian ease, his will is complete: the box at the Albert Hall, the horses, carriages, wines, liquors, provisions, plate, jewellery, collection of Wedgwood china, books, medals, trophies, the house in Portland Place, the stables in Devonshire Mews . . . Maids of twenty-five years service, laboratory assistants and butlers file before us; the most distant relative is not forgotten.

Apart from his publicly lauded achievements in science and industry, Warren possessed another attribute. His will gives ample evidence of an infinite capacity for taking pains with people; in an hierarchical age, when children were born to be seen and not heard, when wives were expected to obey their husbands absolutely, when servants were regarded as possessions and work people taken for granted, it was a rare virtue. For this excellence as much as for any other, his loss was felt for a very long time in Bunhill Row.

# CHAPTER XIV

## *Royal houses*

Lady Longford describes how Queen Victoria in her old age was within sight of public deification – her drum major habitually referred to the day of her accession as 'Ascension Day'. Unquestionably an air of mystique hung over the dumpy person of the Sovereign. Joining in the celebrations of her Golden Jubilee, De La Rue went to endless trouble to perfect the first two-coloured stamps to mark the occasion.

A set of these stamps was carefully mounted and sent to Windsor for the Monarch's inspection. J. S. Purcell, her Controller of Stamps, wrote to acknowledge them:

'I am commanded by the Queen to thank you for the book of Postage Stamps which you have sent to Her Majesty and for giving her notice of the proposed change of design.

The Queen looked at the new stamps but did not give me any opinion upon them.

Perhaps she may do so later'.

Explained the Controller apologetically: 'I am afraid the Queen's mind is more set upon the Churchill incident than upon our stamps'. The Churchill was Lord Randolph, who was then Chancellor of the Exchequer, and one with an attitude of rigid economy. Queen Victoria was waiting breathlessly to see whether he would apply this to the grants for the royal children and grandchildren.

Since Lord Randolph was staying at the Castle when the De La Rue stamp package arrived, it is understandable that the Queen did not give it her attention, for, she said, the Chancellor proceeded to behave 'in a very improper manner'. At dinner he outlined to her the Government's plans for the next session, went up to bed, and 'that vy night in my House, on Windsor paper he deliberately wrote his resignation and sent it to Lord Salisbury', an act which might have toppled the Government and brought back her detested Gladstone. Not until she recovered from the shock could she manage to turn her attention to lesser things, and approve the Jubilee stamp issue.

India asked De La Rue to depict the Queen Empress's head on bi-coloured stamps. The request was made more for reasons of security than of patriotism. The One Rupee had recently been forged rather frequently. In order that the Imperial head should appear to the best advantage, De La Rue submitted 298 different bi-coloured stamp essays, only one of which was to be chosen. If the Queen Empress was unaware of these exertions by her subjects in Bunhill Row, Her Majesty's India Office expressed its appreciation by continuing to award the Company its custom faithfully for the next thirty years.

It was the epoch of jubilees. In 1890 there was even one to commemorate the fiftieth anniversary of Rowland Hill's 1840 Penny Postage. The Post Office asked the Company to produce special Jubilee post cards, 10,000 of which, on sale outside Guildhall, were bought within three hours. Postal workers throughout the country celebrated by giving three loud cheers for the Queen, and enjoyed light refreshments provided by the Postmaster.

*The Times* printed an account of a ceremony which took place at Bunhill Row in connection with the Hill Jubilee. The authorised number of Jubilee envelopes having been printed, the plate was duly broken up in the presence of a number of Inland Revenue and Post Office worthies. The latter were taken on a tour of the works by De La Rue partner W. T. Shaw. Both Warren William and Thomas Andros were conspicuous by their absence. Maybe they thought such a function beneath them, or perhaps the Thomas Andros's were entertaining that day, or one of Warren William's horses was running. Their failure to be present would have been unthinkable in the earlier Thomas's time.

The visitors were told that more than two hundred million adhesive stamps were being produced in Bunhill Row for the State every year. Security arrangements were demonstrated. *The Times* correspondent was impressed by 'the crematorium' for rejected stamps, and by the strict discipline imposed throughout the factories. The Secretary of the Post Office, Sir Arthur Blackwood, concluded a speech with the touching thought that in destroying so beautiful a work of art as that produced by Messrs De La Rue (i.e. the plate for the Jubilee envelopes) 'they were only destroying the seed, and the fruit would remain a thing of beauty and a joy for ever'.

Considering how much De La Rue owed to the Hill family, it was fitting that their contribution of £200 to the Rowland Hill Memorial and Benevolent Fund should be twice as much as anybody else's – exactly double even Lord Rothschild's.

\* \* \*

From the nineties onwards visits to De La Rue became almost *de rigueur* for Queen Victoria's relations. The Duke of Edinburgh was shown round the factories. On another occasion the Duke of York was so intrigued that he stayed not only to luncheon, but tea as well. The Prince and Princess of Wales arrived at a moment's notice to inspect the stamps which De La Rue were printing for the Prince of Wales Hospital Fund. The Prince initialled the first sheet of stamps printed in his presence. *The Times* reported the speech made by Her Royal Highness Princess Alexandra, urging 'the working classes to buy as many as possible', and described how 'the tale of the Princess's sweet words and smiles ran like wildfire' through Bunhill Row. 'Perhaps there was no prettier scene in all the long day than that presented by the bright eager faces of the girls employed, who lined the stairs to get a glimpse of the Royal party as they left'.

*     *     *

In 1896 Warren William fell off his horse in Hyde Park and was never quite the same afterwards. Mildly eccentric at the best of times he now became alarmingly so. He built up an intricate chain supply of umbrellas for himself throughout London, leaving one at Whites, one at the Carlton Club, one at Bunhill Row and others at various restaurants. Going to stay with him was a nerve-wracking business. All over his houses notices were displayed (printed by De La Rue). Since he believed in buying the best in contemporary household equipment, numerous instructions were posted up as to its use. Apprehensive guests in his town house read that if they got stuck in the new lift 'information can be sent by telegraph to the Otis Elevator Company at 4 Queen Victoria Street . . . and if at night to the General Hydraulic Power Company at Blackfriars'. On their descent they might find a poster announcing in big black letters: 'IT IS VERY COLD'. Sometimes they supposed their host to have mistaken them for his race-horses; in the hall of his establishment in York Terrace, Regent's Park, were lists advising them of the distances round the Outer Circle, the Inner Circle, and from the Botanical Gardens to the Conservatory Steps ('OUTER CIRCLE . . . 2 miles, 7 furlongs, 54 yards; ∴ 166 yards short of 3 miles *NB* 5 times round is $14\frac{1}{2}$ miles 50 yards'). He gave similar advice regarding the walk from the hall door to the Piccadilly end of Old Bond Street and the Carlton Club, via Wimpole Street. There was an outcrop of posters concerning his new telephone (the number was Mayfair 5) and his personal telegraphic address (RAINDROPS, LONDON). Among the contingencies covered were alternative arrangements for posting letters when his private post-box was being re-painted. At Newmarket the daily shooting cards read like battle orders; even the coachman's instructions were specially printed.

128

9. Warren William de la Rue,
race-horse owner, by Spy, 1894

Sir Thomas Andros de la Rue, Bt., Chairman
of De La Rue through the Edwardian era,
painted by Fuchs, 1902

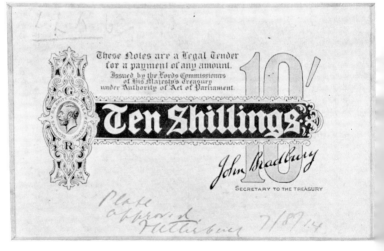

10. British currency notes printed by De La Rue at the outbreak of war 1914, signed by Sir John Bradbury, Permanent Secretary to the Treasury, and consequently known as Bradburys

Visiting valets and maids fared even worse. To avoid disturbing the rest of the house they were told to apply to the de la Rue butler and head housemaid for soft-soled slippers, and be sure to serve morning tea 'in the little pots provided for the purpose'. If visitors did not receive a satisfactory response to their bell-pulling, they were advised 'to ring three times for Mr de la Rue'. Below stairs there was a feast of information ranging from leaflets for making Dr Kussmaul's Fattening Porridge, to hints for working Baker's Patent Decker Oven. The hall boy was given a printed reminder about *The Maintenance of the Bicycle*, the key of which he was to keep in his pocket, 'and not hide it or leave it around'.

His neighbours found themselves inundated with printed suggestions. Being the oldest resident of York Terrace he began bombarding the other inmates as to whom to complain to about early milk carts, or why to favour the Akonia Process of Dust Prevention. Not infrequently his requests were benevolent. He urged that generous Christmas Boxes be given to the Garden Night Watchman ('a most reliable man continually controlling the Gardens in all weathers'), as well as donations to the Cabmen's Shelter Fund. Although most of his house regulations were for the comfort of himself and his visitors, he also besought the servants to take precaution against 'the cold coming up through the waste-pipe', so that they should not be discomforted whilst bathing in the servants' bathroom.

Poor Warren William grew stranger and stranger. We do not know whether he retired voluntarily from the senior partnership, or whether his younger brother, Thomas Andros, employed forceful persuasion. At any rate he went off to his house in Tenby where a comprehensive table of the Welsh tides was specially drawn up for his benefit, and where he eventually killed himself by coal-gas poisoning. The unceasing diligence which he had always displayed was a quality which was to be noticeably absent amongst the new rulers of Bunhill Row.

# CHAPTER XV

# Sir Thomas Andros de la Rue:
## The ivory tower

Thomas Andros was left in command. Straight away he changed the firm from a partnership to a private company, with himself as chairman; and then, keeping pace with the current trend, in 1898 he decided that De La Rue should be a public company. That same year his work as principal Governor of the Royal Chest Hospital was rewarded with a baronetcy. 'Cherchez la verité' became his motto. It is said that a similar honour was about to be conferred on Warren at the time of his death. With his record of service to science, together with the part he played in furthering British business relations abroad, the baronetcy would have fallen more deservedly on father than on son.

Although the firm was now a public company, the de la Rue family and its friends still owned nearly all the shares and it was, in fact, a dictatorship ruled by Thomas Andros. He quarrelled with his younger brother Ernest, who as a result left Bunhill Row and later joined the board of His Master's Voice. A greater loss was the retirement of Dr Hugo Müller. His chemical expertise, which did so much to put the firm ahead in the printing world, was sadly lacking under the new regime.

Thomas Andros was not a stupid man. If only fortune had frowned upon him occasionally, instead of maintaining a fixed smile, all might have been well. But he could never remember a time when he had not been surrounded by prosperity. Unlike his ancestors he was not hardened to the cut and thrust of the business world. It had all been too easy for him. The impetus created jointly by the drive of his father, Colonel Billy, and Dr Müller, was of such strength that it carried the firm a considerable distance into the twentieth century. Basking in their reflected glories Thomas Andros mistook their achievements for his own. His trouble was that he inherited too big a success, and did not know what to do with it.

He was by no means lazy. He had shown that he could work hard, and even display a self control worthy of his father, Warren. He was particularly able in his handling of an episode with a peevish Commissioner of British Central Africa, Sir Harry Johnston. Instead of entrusting the stamp affairs of his Protectorate to the Crown Agents, as was customary, Sir Harry tried to deal with them himself. Moreover he insisted that De La Rue should employ his own stamp design, which depicted two negroes with pick and shovel standing self-consciously on a map of Africa; beside them was a coffee tree in full bearing, and underneath, the motto: 'Light in Darkness'.

Thomas Andros listened patiently while Sir Harry, in his ignorance, made endless objections to the submitted designs: 'What I dislike about D is having the motto at the sides . . . If, without interfering with the map of Africa, you could squeeze in the motto "Light in Darkness" along the top . . .' he continued, exhorting Thomas Andros to take care that 'the rivers and lakes are engraved as on my original design . . .' and all this on something the size of a postage stamp. To his credit Thomas Andros accepted the instructions about the rivers and lakes, but regretted the impossibility of finishing the proofs before Sir Harry left for Africa as the works would be shut for Christmas. He also ventured to suggest that Sir Harry's idea of having a black stamp over-printed in black would not make for distinctness.

Displeased by this gentlest of criticisms of an idea which was unbelievably stupid, Sir Harry retaliated with an additional demand: 'If there is any space underneath the motto, instead of filling it with some unmeaning dot or star, put in a minute Scottish thistle'. Refraining from telling Sir Harry to take his thistle to hell, Thomas Andros wrote on Christmas Eve to give his private address in Cadogan Square in case he might wish to contact him over the holiday.

When the finished stamps reached Africa, Sir Harry inevitably found every fault. 'I am very much dissatisfied with the way in which Messrs De La Rue have carried out this contract', he grumbled. Why couldn't he have stamps like those being manufactured by Bradbury Wilkinson for the British South Africa Company? This was unfair, as Thomas Andros restrainedly pointed out to the Crown Agents, who by now were umpiring the contest. Sir Harry, he explained, having wanted the whole issue printed on a shoe string, had ordered the stamps to be produced lithographically, the cheapest of all methods, which could not possibly give results comparable with those of Bradbury, using expensive copperplate.

With intermittent rumbles Sir Harry's wrath subsided. He even conceded that his design *had* been a little complicated. Having come in like a lion, he went out like a spring lamb: 'Let us leave this subject for the present', he wrote 'and turn to the hawthorn coming into bloom and the lilac bushes in full flower everywhere'. De La Rue went on to print further issues for his Protectorate, and Thomas Andros had demonstrated how to succeed with a difficult customer while really trying.

After he became supreme commander of the Company, however, Sir Thomas Andros de la Rue did not sustain performances of this kind. He continued to be regular enough in his hours of attendance at Bunhill Row. You could set your watch by the time of his arrival at 10.30 each morning and his departure at 4. Such punctuality was indeed exemplary in so wealthy a man, at any rate in one with so pronounced a taste for the *haut monde*. Once he had arrived in his office, though, his work people felt him to be less approachable than the Deity. He always wore a high hat, black frock coat and striped trousers. When he made a tour of the factories, accompanied by the works managers, word was sent on ahead so that all hands might be on their best behaviour. They never saw him address anyone. 'He was a reserved kind of man', they said. Even his own sons always called him 'The Guv'nor'.

To a collector of beautiful things, as Thomas Andros was, the environs of Bunhill Row were not an attractive sight. He himself had a fine office in what was once his grandfather's private house, but he must have been aware, like his receptionist, Alfred Lane, of 'the terrible slums that existed behind and beside our works in Bunhill Row right up to Whitecross Street – the squalor, filth and conditions in which people lived like animals'.

The welfare of adjacent areas was not Thomas Andros's concern. In any case the Peabody Trust came forward to try to clear them up. But working conditions in the De La Rue factories were his responsibility and he did nothing to modernise them. Nellie Cockram's earliest memory as a playing card packer was of 'very old floorboards and cupboards round the walls, everything seemed very old to me'. The women's lavatories were little more than holes in the ground, which two labourers cleared twice a week. Paid holidays were unheard of, and there was great excitement when five whole days off were granted to any staff who had been with the Company over ten years. The lead given by the Company in factory welfare, which had so delighted the visiting journalists in the 1850s, disappeared after the turn of the century. Little progress was made in this field until after the first world war. Nobody was actually ill treated, but a note of cynicism crept into the workers' loyalties. They had no illusions, for instance, about the intensive new fire precautions. Privately they registered the thought that these were not enforced to safeguard them so much as to impress the Government and to keep Government contracts.

Nor did the wages increase. A De La Rue woman worker in the coming Edwardian era was paid the same as her counterpart in 1857: the top rate was 12s a week. Frederick Bagley's wages as a boy in 1900 were 7s for a 54 hour week. To those at the top of the heirarchy Thomas Andros could be quite generous. He once sent for David Turner, an engraver, complimented him on a fine piece of work for stamp heads and pressed a £5 note into his hand. But unlike Warren or Colonel Billy, it did not occur to him to worry about the well-being of lesser De La Rue fry.

*　　　*　　　*

When Thomas Andros took over as Supervisor of Colonial Printing, the sort of thing that went to his head was the Ceylonese affair. The Crown Agents confided to De La Rue that they were having some trouble with Ceylon, who repeatedly sent them ambiguous demands. Their correspondence was getting out of hand. 'Does telegram 27 November specify all postal requirements Instructions conflict', wired the bewildered Crown Agents. They received an unfathomable Ceylonese reply: 'Referring to your telegram of 2nd January my telegram ordering (? orders) by telegraph what is requisite pending preparation new dies my letter of 7th November subsequent quarterly instalments'. Helplessly the Crown Agents turned to De La Rue. 'We should be glad of any remarks which your experience of this country may lead you to think would be of use to the Government of Ceylon', they appealed.

Thomas Andros gave the benefit of his advice. In return the firm received a new order to print stamps for Ceylon. Because so much time had been wasted the Crown Agents wished to speed up the work. Carried away by the sound of his own voice, however, Thomas Andros was still pontificating about colour. The Crown Agents felt that they had asked for advice, not a sermon. An unprecedented note of friction crept into the hitherto genial relations between them and Bunhill Row. The exchange of letters ended sharply.

When negotiations were started for Trinidad stamps, Crown Agent Blake was still smarting from the scrap over Ceylon. He declared apprehensively to Thomas Andros: 'I am most anxious that the stamp work should go smoothly and to avoid any recurrence of the kind of correspondence which we had last winter'. Mr Blake then gathered up enough courage to write firmly to De La Rue: 'I return herewith the designs for the Uganda stamps and I am sorry to say that they will not do'.

These warning signals should have wiped the complacent smile off the Company's face; there was no lasting guarantee that the eye of the Crown Agents, or indeed of the Inland Revenue, might not wander to other printing companies. The Crown Agents were already much taken with Waterlow copperplate printed stamps. But when the Colonies looked longingly in the direction of copperplate printing, the Company addressed them in the manner of a lazy and overbearing governess dealing with rather difficult children. The Crown Agents were told that they must continue with letterpress without more ado – Thomas Andros considered that letterpress printing (with Dr Müller's fugitive inks) had been good enough for De La Rue's previous contracts, and he saw no reason why the *status quo* should not continue. To call his attitude a *folie de grandeur* might at this stage be to exaggerate. But there was no question that he was over-confident of his firm's superiority.

An unnecessary piece of high-mindedness on the part of De La Rue occurred with the death of the old Queen, whose prayer to be spared a little time in which to view the new century was granted. She died on January 22nd 1901. On January 29th, the Crown Agents received a business-like telegram from St Lucia. The island wanted to enquire about new halfpenny and one penny stamps. On being consulted about designs for these, the Company, quite as though it enjoyed the private ear of the new monarch, replied: 'It will be impossible to do anything regarding the new plates until His Majesty the King has settled which likeness of himself he wishes to appear, and we hardly think he is likely to attend to such matters for another week or two'.

When Edward VII eventually approved the De La Rue designs for the British stamps, India and most of the Colonies, Thomas Andros perceived an endless vista of prosperity stretching ahead, and he was reluctant to risk disturbing it. The idea of diversifying into other fields, or of trying to improve upon the firm's current printing processes, did not appeal to him. He liked things the way they were. He felt that God was in his Edwardian heaven and all was right with his Company's world. He was the absolute ruler of the little empire in Bunhill Row and very much the head of the de la Rue family. His three sons, Evelyn, Ivor and Stuart, now arrived on the scene, entering the Works rather in the spirit of a Prince of Wales being presented to his people.

# CHAPTER XVI

## *Looking glass house*

'The great art of riding', said the White Knight to Alice, 'is keeping your balance . . . The more head downwards I am the more I keep inventing things', he added, as she delivered him out of a ditch. Evelyn de la Rue was not content to ride a horse like other people either. A more accomplished equestrian than the White Knight, he would nevertheless cause consternation when out hunting with the Whaddon Chase by his custom of holding on to the pommel of his saddle and vaulting over the fences.

Of all the de la Rues, who were an inventive family, Evelyn, the eldest son of Thomas Andros, most resembled Lewis Carroll's strange and charming creature: in some ways he outdid the White Knight, who would have been proud to have fathered some of Evelyn's more improbable patents (which varied from a recipe for making rocking horses move forward to one for keeping tennis balls white). For the young he held the same kind of benignly eccentric fascination. Once he went too far, and decorated the tree for a Christmas party with live birds and little animals in cages; these were not received with satisfaction by the smaller guests, and had to be returned to Gamages.

Like the White Knight there was more than a touch of pathos about him. He wrote a book of verse for children, illustrated by Victor Venner, and published by De La Rue. Unhappily it turned out to be too old for children and too young for grown ups. While still at Eton, and at Cambridge where he read chemistry, his mind teemed with projects which were seldom destined to thrive. The

137

cruellest disappointment of all was the publication of his thesis on the creation of matter. It contained his ideas about the theory of relativity, and was to have been his *magnum opus* but Einstein decided to produce his at the same time, which somewhat overshadowed it. One of Evelyn's daughters made the loyal understatement: 'they both drew parallel conclusions but Einstein's simply-worded book attracted public attention'.

Although Evelyn respected his father he had little in common with him. Sir Thomas Andros's ideal evening was a Gilbert and Sullivan first night, followed by a large soirée in Cadogan Square. The theatre became his great interest. The St James's Theatre, according to his grandchildren, was kept alive largely by his support. He and his wife, Emily, knew all the leading actors and actresses of the day who lent the Cadogan Square parties a dashingly theatrical air. Invitations were much sought after, particularly for the big fancy dress balls. There was one on the eve of Evelyn's wedding, when everyone appeared in elaborate costumes except for the actor-manager, Sir George Alexander, who arrived with telling effect in ordinary evening dress and a paper frill round his little finger, crying: 'I am a cutlet'. These theatrical friends, including Sir George, were enlisted into supporting the London Chest Hospital, of which Sir Thomas was still the conscientious Governor.

All this glitter was not for Evelyn. He was brought up in the country by Speed relations of his mother, who lived comfortably enough. Having inherited the Leyland Shipping line, Aunt Eleanor Speed reputedly handed it over to a young man called John Ellerman to run, with the words: 'Now I am going to give you your chance'.

*　　　*　　　*

Evelyn enjoyed country life, and chose a country bride, May Franklin, the handsome daughter of a squire who lived in Nottinghamshire and hunted with five packs of hounds. Squire

Franklin was much respected in his country. Family history
relates how he once took a train home from London and arrived
back at his manor house to find a posse of police outside. A detec-
tive in Piccadilly mistook him for Jack the Ripper, tracked him to
Nottingham, and was more than a little embarrassed when his
quarry was apologetically visited by the Chief Constable.

Evelyn went to the office every day as he and his brothers had
done since they came down from Cambridge. Old Bunhill Row
hands have sunny memories of the three boys rushing up the stairs
wearing their panama hats. Unfortunately the relationship between Evelyn, Ivor and Stuart was anything but sunny. Whenever Sir Thomas's back was turned quarrels broke out between
them.

To begin with Evelyn and May had a house in Westbourne
Terrace, Hyde Park, where great-grandfather Thomas had lived.
But subsequently, in order to get away from the bickering in
Bunhill Row, Evelyn and his horsey, uncomplicated wife took to
living in country houses which were usually large, beautiful,
Elizabethan and in Hertfordshire. From these Evelyn commuted
to the City, once walking in order to prove to himself that it could
be done. He was inclined to forget that, for the most part, the
houses were rented, and absentmindedly spent large sums im-
proving them, adding stables, garages, servants' wings or model
farms. From his airy approach to his own affairs it can be deduced
that he was not a financier.

He returned to his Tudor homes so depressed from De La Rue,
where his father tended to laugh at his suggestions, and his
brothers to lose their tempers with him, that he frequently went
straight to his workshop and got on with his cabinet making.
Sensitive and highly-strung, he was the opposite of hearty, hard-
riding May who never knew a day's illness, and could not grasp
what agonies her husband underwent in Bunhill Row. She was
late for meals and uninterested in her cooks' art. As their domestic

muddles grew Evelyn took increasing refuge in his hobbies. His delight in motor cars was as total as that of Toad of Toad Hall. Dreaming like him of a motor car which went 'Poop Poop', he invented a horn which was attached to the steering wheel. It was called the 'Eural' horn, 'Eur' being Rue spelt backwards. Lovingly he registered upon various devices every mile run by his two Rolls Royces and a station wagon called Iris ('I Run in Silence').

\*     \*     \*

There was one invention, however, which Evelyn was convinced should be developed by the firm. This was the fountain pen. Even Sir Thomas Andros admired the persistence of his son who took out no less than seventeen patents on the subject. For once Evelyn was allowed his way.

Like so many things connected with Evelyn the events which led to the birth of the famous Onoto pen were somewhat bizarre. There was at that time a female impersonator on roller skates by the name of George Sweetser, who also chanced to be an inventor. He too had a fixation about pens. Already on the market in 1905 there was a model of German origin called the 'Pelican' which, when depressed, sucked up ink. The drawback to this, perceived Mr Sweetser, was that if the plunger was *accidentally* depressed 'you got either a pocketful of ink or a shower of black rain' . . . He went to work and turned out another model, which he thought 'mighty good', and he made an appointment to demonstrate it in Bunhill Row.

When he was over eighty and still roller skating vigorously, George Sweetser recalled the interview in a magazine article: 'The stuffing was completely knocked out of me when the gentleman I saw, Sir Evelyn (then Mr) de la Rue pulled out of his pocket an exactly similar pen, his own invention of a month or so prior date to mine . . .' After the initial shock the two White Knights recovered themselves. Mr Sweetser did not, he said, think much of Mr de la Rue's invention, not, he hastened to point out, because

of sour grapes. 'Oh dear no! but because the filling was a fumble as
the piston had to be given four single strokes and the rod twisted
twice to engage and disengage the piston' . . . very Evelyn-esque.
Mr Sweetser graciously allowed that his visit to Bunhill Row was
a blessing in disguise, because if his pen 'had not been anticipated
the great Onoto would never have been born'.

To remedy the faults in his model and challenged by Evelyn's
which so closely resembled it, Mr Sweetser purchased an eight-
penny 'Houndsditch' pen, converted it and hurried back to Bunhill
Row to see the same gentleman. 'When I pushed the plunger down
he saw the ink go down in the bottle so knew it must have gone
up into the pen'. It was a moving moment. Evelyn uttered the
historic words: 'I like that', which as Mr Sweetser pointed out,
was not a wise admission. 'If I had been of a certain persuasion the
price might have been doubled'. It was evident that Evelyn
wanted the pen badly. He asked the cost, said 'I will have it', and
Mr Sweetser came out 'ten minutes after going in, with a big fat
cheque'.

This episode may reveal only too clearly that Evelyn's method
of negotiating a deal was anything but businesslike. But his in-
spiration proved to be right. Mr Sweetser's pen was a good investment. Having convinced his father that at last he was on to something worthwhile, Evelyn was allowed to spend the vast sum of
£50,000 on advertising the pen. It was called the 'Onoto' for the
only reason that its pronunciation was the same in all languages.
This publicity campaign was the one investment of any note
authorised in the reign of Sir Thomas Andros.

Under the onslaught of such intensive advertising the country
quickly capitulated, and the Onoto became what it was pro-
claimed to be: *the* pen. Unwilling to be left out Mr Sweetser made
some unusual claims on behalf of his invention. 'It can', he stressed,
'not only be filled in a flash and written with, but could be used to
syringe your ears, spray the geraniums with insecticide, and it is

ideal for 'ink-splashers' as it will carry across the road'. Could one ask more of a pen?

\*　　　\*　　　\*

For Thomas Andros the spacious Edwardian days rolled comfortably on. He was blissfully unaware of impending disaster. Had he looked, the tip of the iceburg was plain to see – the possibility of the printing contracts for all British stamps not being renewed; the thought that these might not be automatically reawarded to De La Rue did not cross his mind. The firm had been printing the stamps for the last thirty years, and Thomas Andros had completely forgotten the public outcry in the eighties over the De La Rue monopoly.

Looking back it is hard to understand the de la Rues' utter certainty that this controversy would never recur. They made no special efforts to maintain their contracts. In spite of decreased manufacturing costs they continued to put in the same prices, thereby making colossal profits. They behaved as if the contracts were a foregone conclusion, and theirs by right. A later chairman of De La Rue believes that Thomas Andros only allowed the Onoto to be developed because it diverted attention from the fortune which the Company was making out of stamp printing.

The inevitable storm devastated the de la Rues, bursting from a sky which to them had seemed eternally blue. There are varied accounts as to how it happened; the firm was either so confounded by loss of face, or so ashamed by the amount of its previous profits, that no actual record was kept. The known facts are these. Mindful of past accusations regarding a De La Rue monopoly, and suspecting that modern machinery ought to be producing stamps at lower prices, the Inland Revenue proposed in 1911 to split the contract, awarding the higher denominations to De La Rue and the lower (and more profitable) ones to Harrisons. The latter were hereditary printers to the Sovereign but had never printed a stamp in their lives.

To Thomas Andros this was galling; De La Rue, the Goliath of the letterpress printing world, was being slain by an untried David. When he was sent for by the Secretary of the Post Office he is supposed to have retorted that he would see everyone damned before he would share any contract, and to have stormed furiously out of the room with the parting shot that De La Rue would accept all or nothing. They got nothing because the Government gave the entire contract to Harrisons.

Another version has it that the Secretary of the Post Office asked Sir Thomas Andros if he could make a slight reduction in prices in order to satisfy the Board of Inland Revenue, and received a categoric 'no' in reply. The short-sightedness of the De La Rue attitude was pathetic. If the firm had made even a small concession it could have retained the contract indefinitely, and still enjoyed ample prosperity.

The tragedy was that the Harrison proofs turned out to be far from satisfactory. At their first try Harrisons could not hope to equal the expertise gained by De La Rue over more than half a century. If only Thomas Andros had exercised a modicum of patience, the superiority of *his* stamps over the Harrison ones, as soon as they appeared under joint contract, would have been obvious. Having cleared itself of monopoly charges, the Government would then have had no alternative but to give back all the stamp orders to De La Rue.

Instead the firm lost them for ever. The blow killed Thomas Andros. He died only a few months later without recovering from the shock. Happily for him he did not live to see the Harrison stamps issued. The bitter pill of perpetually posting letters with someone else's stamps on them would have been hard to swallow.

# CHAPTER XVII

## *A house divided against itself*

The mighty were indeed fallen. The loss of the Inland Revenue orders had all kinds of repercussions for De La Rue which ought to have chastened its management. The loss of public face was bad enough, but inside the private world of Bunhill Row there were further problems – redundant men, idle factory spaces. Half the maintenance men had to be dismissed. The Saint Works were closed down.

The blow could have been a challenge if the de la Rues had chosen to interpret it as such. The firm could have fought back but its leadership appeared to be paralysed. It required a strong business head to readjust the economic balance; unfortunately there was no longer anyone of sufficient calibre left in Bunhill Row to rise to the occasion.

Together with the India order, the Inland Revenue contracts accounted for half the firm's production figures and employment of labour. The world should have been scoured to replace the loss. But unlike their forebears, the twentieth century de la Rues did not venture far afield. It is uncertain whether they ever got as far as Calais on business.

\*     \*     \*

Alas, poor Evelyn: although he succeeded as chairman, financially the business was left equally among the three brothers; trying to keep the peace between them presented him with endless difficulties. Stuart and Ivor were rarely united behind him. In addition he had to face an unforeseen and disagreeable develop-

11. *Left* Sidney Lamert, *right* Bernard Westall (Mayfair Cartoons, 'Spy' Series) first chairmen of the Company to be appointed outside the de la Rue family

12. British Industries Fair, 1937: H.M. King George VI, H.M. Queen Elizabeth and H.R.
the Duke of Kent, being shown the De La Rue stand by Bernard Westall

ment in the Works concerning his father's will. At his death, with a fortune of three quarters of a million, Thomas Andros was the wealthiest of the de la Rues. He left not only money, but many treasures: good pictures, including some Bassanos and an Andrea del Sarto, antiques, and magnificent jewellery. Each member of the family was allowed to pick an item. Evelyn chose a tiara copied from the Tsarina's. Some annuities were also left to managers, engravers and foremen of De La Rue.

Just before Christmas 1911, the will was published in the newspapers. A rumour spread round Bunhill Row that not only these men, but all De La Rue employees, would benefit according to years of service. Never had the festive season seemed brighter. Expectations ran high while Sir Thomas of happy memory was gratefully toasted. Nellie Cockram in the playing card department was moved to exclaim: 'I am like the disbelieving Thomas in the Bible, until I have that money in my hand I shall not believe'. So great was the astonishment that the sorting department passed round a hat for contributions to enable two women sorters to take the afternoon off, and go to Somerset House to check up. On their arrival an exasperated official asked them how many more people would be wanting to know the details of Sir Thomas Andros's will. Inquiries from De La Rue had been pouring in all day.

It was all too good to be true. The papers, including *The Times*, had been misconstrued. It was only Sir Thomas Andros's household employees, not those of the firm, who were to benefit. The two women from the sorting department slipped disconsolately back into Bunhill Row with the dampening news. There the holiday mood was still in the air. Groups of workers, as yet unenlightened, stood around digesting the idea of a communal windfall. No one felt like work. A hush descended when the word went round that Sir Evelyn, the new chief, had arrived on the scene. He had the unsavoury task of explaining the mistake, and was brusque in his nervousness. As the muttering men and women returned to their jobs, the image of the late Sir Thomas Andros changed swiftly from that of a benevolent old gentleman into something far less printable.

It was a testing time for the de la Rues, who were openly accused of swindling these work-people out of their deserts. To proceed as if nothing untoward had occurred was practically impossible. As Tommy Green, who was then a clerk in Bunhill Row, commented: 'In some ways it would have been better for the de la Rue family to have paid out these folk, for they never had any luck with their inheritance'. Ensuing events proved him to be right. Outwardly, nevertheless, the firm mourned the passing of its chairman. The annual outing to Clacton was cancelled, and all communications were sent out on notepaper bearing the thickest of black borders.

A rider to the loss of the Inland Revenue orders was provided by the new monarch, King George V, himself a keen and knowledgeable philatelist. He sent for Evelyn aboard the the royal yacht at Cowes, and deplored the new Harrison stamp proofs. 'Make me look like a stuffed monkey don't they?' he demanded crossly. Wretchedly Evelyn was forced to admit they did, but that there was nothing he could do about it.

\*　　　\*　　　\*

Meanwhile Evelyn had been secretly cherishing the idea of designing a motor car. His father's fortune now offered him the means of turning his dream into a reality. He could not resist the temptation. Instead of reinvesting Sir Thomas Andros's money in De La Rue, whence it came, he entered into an association with a Mr Taunton, who shared his enthusiasm for the motor car project – understandably, since Evelyn was prepared to finance everything. Together they evolved a prototype called 'the Taunton'. They set up a factory in Liège, and intended to sweep the European market. The first cars, selling like hot cakes, were being ordered before they were even completed, and success was almost within their grasp when disaster overtook Evelyn yet again: World War I broke out. Belgium was invaded, the Liège factory was appropriated by the Germans, and Evelyn lost £80,000. As the Bunhill Row clerk said, they never did have any luck with their inheritance.

# CHAPTER XVIII

## *All fall down*

Once upon a time there were three brothers. The two eldest were brave and good, but the youngest was very difficult. They lived in a castle in the city. Sometimes the youngest brother daydreamed how nice it would be if his brothers went away and he was king of the castle. One day his eldest brother went off to fight in the wars; his country needed him. Then his second brother went off to fight, and the third brother laughed because now he *was* king of the castle. While the others were away he bought up more castles, ruined ones at bargain prices, and by the time they came back he had spent everything in the counting house. So they had to sell their castle and did not live happily ever after. Such, briefly, was the cautionary tale of Stuart de la Rue.

Shortly after war was declared in 1914 Evelyn was posted to the Ministry of Munitions. In an effort to escape from this appointment he promptly wrote to the Colonel of the East Kent Yeomanry, who was his wife's cousin, Lord Guilford. When the regiment was mobilised Evelyn managed to join it, complete with his own chargers and groom. He was later observed sitting knitting unconcernedly in the trenches while under intense fire at Paschendaele and Ypres. He said he occupied his mind by inventing a machine for winding knitting wool. Fervently patriotic, when his youngest child was born he named him Victor for victory and St George for England. His second brother, Ivor, enlisted in 1915, and demonstrated his own form of courage by refusing a commission until he felt ready to give military commands. The manner in which he gave orders at Bunhill Row had always been considered unequivocal. When a De La Rue employee came across him digging trenches on Salisbury Plain in the guise of the lowest form of army life, a tommy, he pondered the fact and found it endearing.

*    *    *

The outbreak of the Great War brought the firm a brief moment of glory. One of the first reactions anticipated by the British Government was a run on gold reserves. It ordered all gold sovereigns to be handed in, and for the first twenty-four hours after England's ultimatum to Germany had expired at midnight on August 4th, postal orders were used as currency. On August 5th De La Rue received a letter from H.M. Stationery Office requesting the firm to 'manufacture 10s Treasury Notes with notepaper supplied by the Inland Revenue . . .'

A simple design was hurriedly composed in Bunhill Row and its proof submitted on 6th August. Notice of approval was received by De La Rue on 7th August after Bunhill Row had finished work for the day. When they got home all the foremen found a telegram from Stuart de la Rue awaiting them: 'Your services required urgently if possible all night present yourself Star Gate as soon as possible'. The firm suspended its other business, and the Factory Act was specially waived by the Home Secretary. Every man, woman, girl and boy in Bunhill Row worked night and day in eight hour shifts to deliver $2\frac{1}{2}$ million notes to Somerset House during the first five weeks of the war. De La Rue also designed a £1 note which was the same as the 10s, only slightly larger and in black. But the order to print this was given to Waterlow Brothers and Leighton (then no connection of Waterlow and Sons except that the original Waterlows of the two firms were cousins). Having just gone to war, H.M.G. had more important things to think about than the fairness of its domestic printing contracts. Stuart de la Rue, however, considered he had been slighted. War or no war, he insisted on protesting loudly to the Stationery Office that

149

whereas Waterlow Brothers and Leighton were printing all the £1 notes, De La Rue was having to share the 10s. When it came to the second issue the Government obediently reversed the roles; De La Rue alone printed the £1, while sharing the 10s with Waterlow Brothers and Leighton.

Wartime exigencies thus brought about the introduction of the modern English currency note. The golden sovereign became, like the Pax Britannica itself, a thing of the past.

The next part of the story has a moral in its tail. Both De La Rue and Waterlow and Sons (as opposed to Waterlow Brothers and Leighton) realised that the hastily prepared English notes of the early wartime issues must be replaced with something offering greater protection against forgery. Edgar Waterlow and Stuart de la Rue put their heads together. They decided that if the Government gave the contract for the next English banknotes to De La Rue (to be printed by letterpress) the latter would slip Waterlow and Sons a shilling for every thousand notes, and conversely if Waterlows were asked to print (by copperplate) they would pay 6d a thousand to De La Rue, the copperplate method of production being more expensive.

To their joint chagrin neither of them won. H.M.G. gave the entire contract to Waterlow Brothers and Leighton to be printed by a third process, newer and cheaper, called 'photogravure' with which the other two firms were unfamiliar. Waterlow Brothers and Leighton were not familiar with it either, having stumbled across the new process by pure chance. Their managing director happened to have a brother-in-law in the Stationery Office, who had heard that a process called 'photogravure' was being developed by the Sun Engraving Co. Why, he suggested, did they not put it forward as an alternative process to that of De La Rue and Waterlow & Sons?

Beaten by a comparatively minor competitor, one would have thought that De La Rue, who had printed their first banknote fifty-seven years earlier, could have persevered and found some means of reversing the Government's decision. Had Stuart not taken the lazy course of conspiring with Edgar Waterlow, Bunhill Row could have retained the English currency note contracts for another decade. It was a short-sighted move.

*   *   *

When Evelyn went off to join the East Kent Yeomanry he had done so feeling that De La Rue was left in the adequate hands of his brother Ivor. He did not foresee that Ivor would soon follow him into the army, leaving thirty-two year old Stuart in entire charge of Bunhill Row.

The Company started the war with £90,000 to its credit. By 1918 it had achieved the rare distinction of being £90,000 in debt – most other firms of comparable size having thriven on the war-time boom. De La Rue had been making munitions in the form of shell caps, and still executed the massive Indian stamp and stationery orders. Notwithstanding, Stuart managed to plunge the Company into a chain-reaction of disaster.

Lloyd George was insistent that manufacturing firms should diversify. Stuart needed no urging. With fine abandon he acquired a collection of concerns which bore no relation to each other, and none to De La Rue; the only common denominator was the precarious state of their finances. His purchases ranged from the Philip Mead cricket bat to the Clyno car. Motors, it seemed, were a family obsession. It was ironic that two of the items he bought which got nowhere under his leadership, the one a boiler business, and the other a small plastics affair, were precursors of the firm's stalwarts of today, Potterton's and Formica Limited.

Stuart de la Rue appears to have been a Janus. On the one hand there was Stuart the hapless businessman, unreliable, even un-balanced. There was also the Stuart of good works, the Hertford-shire J.P., the Governor of the Royal Chest Hospital (in succession to Sir Thomas Andros), the family man (four boys and a girl), married to the daughter of a K.C. with the resounding name of Alexander Dundas Ogilvie Wedderburn.

The twentieth century de la Rue brothers had embarked on their commercial careers with every material advantage. But whereas Evelyn had business disasters subsequently thrust upon him, Stuart seemed to court them assiduously. His method of conducting De La Rue affairs resulted in trouble at every turn. In a misguided effort, for instance, to prove the inferiority of a Waterlow Brothers and Leighton note, he ordered one to be copied in Bunhill Row. He then presented this counterfeit note at a bank, where it was accepted without question as genuine. Thrilled by the success of this manoeuvre, Stuart informed the Government authorities. To his astonishment he narrowly escaped a term of imprisonment for forgery.

When Ivor de la Rue returned from the war he suffered a nervous breakdown and did not re-enter the firm. Evelyn, on his demobilisation, was glad of a chance to be able to devote himself to his own affairs. In any case Stuart had made it perfectly clear that he intended to continue running De La Rue without fraternal assistance. This suited Evelyn well enough. Unexpectedly soldiering had proved to be his *métier*. The comradeship dispelled his formerly brusque shyness, and from the point of view of the human touch in Bunhill Row, it was a pity he did not reappear there. But he was busy with other things. In connection with his ravaged motor car factory at Liège, he was campaigning against Lloyd George's indifferent attitude to private compensation. His mind also dwelt frequently on his army days. He managed to persuade his wife away from her horses and spent some time conducting her round the recent battlefields, insisting that she write an account of the tour for their parish magazine. As she had been brought up on the hunting field and not in the school-room, her original notes make interesting reading. 'We arrived at Ostend to find France (*sic*) in ruins ... I noticed that the Fort on the right was called 'pommes à vendre' and the one on the left 'défense d'uriner'.

While Evelyn was engaged in family pursuits, and Ivor in re-covering his health, Stuart was getting into deep waters. Until 1921 he kept the rest of the family in ignorance of the firm's parlous state. Then he dropped his bombshell. The Company, he announced, was just about destitute. His relations were horror-struck. Although many other family businesses were in the process of being bought up, the de la Rues, thanks to Stuart's silence, had no inkling that their own was verging on total ruin.

There was even worse to come. That same year the Inchcape Commission was set up to see what could be done to improve the lot of India. As a result the Government approached De La Rue about the possibility of manufacturing India's printing require-ments *in situ* on the sub-continent, and not in Bunhill Row. The effort of setting up in India was unthinkable to Stuart. Just as his father, Thomas Andros, had flatly refused to compromise over the Inland Revenue orders and lost them for ever, Stuart now made the same mistake. Consequently the India order, the Company's remaining anchor, was soon lost. Twentieth century de la Rues had the same inexorable capacity for sowing the seeds of their own destruction as central figures in Greek tragedy.

Though De La Rue was faltering, some personnel from Waterlow and Sons sought new positions in Bunhill Row. That anyone should leave healthy Waterlow for sickly De La Rue seems extraordinary. The reason was that Stuart had recently appointed as his managing director an ex-Waterlow chief called Albert Gronow, a Welshman whose methods of business were as peculiar as his own. Mr Gronow proceeded to offer the incentive of a directorship in De La Rue to Harold Rapkin, currently head of Waterlow's printing department, on condition that he brought with him certain key men. These key men included Waterlow's head designer and engraver, as well as the chief engineer who was in the midst of perfecting a rotary printing machine.

Mr Rapkin and his men accepted Mr Gronow's proposal. Trailing somewhat aimlessly in their wake came a junior clerk by the name of Bernard Westall, who thought he might as well join the exodus and accompany Mr Rapkin, whose daughter he happened recently to have married. This junior clerk was destined to change the course of De La Rue history.

The dismayed De La Rue staff watched the influx from Waterlow like the inmates of a war-impoverished city viewing the arrival of a horde of refugees. There were these additional mouths to feed on their scanty rations. The inevitable backbiting in Bunhill Row became fierce and widespread.

Unfortunately Mr Gronow was so engrossed by internal cliques, and counter-cliques, that he had no time to appreciate the desperateness of the firm's position. Once filled with the most up-to-date security printing plant in the world, the Bunhill Row factories now contained obsolescent junk. Letterpress machines in the Anchor Works were antiquated and idle save for the production of some badly printed East African and Malayan notes. No one in authority at Bunhill Row recognised that as a mode of security printing, letterpress was dead.

A curious relic lay mouldering in the basement of the Star Works. In Victorian times pure gum arabic had been expensive and at Warren's request Hugo Müller devised a means of producing cheaper Gatti gum. A weird and complicated apparatus was involved. To purify the Gatti gum, which came from the bark of trees and contained small pieces of wood, Dr Müller mixed the gum with water in the Star Works basement and had it pumped up to a tank on the roof. Thence it was piped by gravity down to the basement again. The mixture was then strained through cloth cylinders, having gained sufficient strength in the course of its fall to force its way through the closely woven material. Once more the mixture went up to the roof, once more it came down, this time to the gumming department in the George Works' basement. In spite of the fact that the price of Gatti gum had soared the same ancient process was still pursuing its weary way in 1922. In the basement of the Dufferin Works a superannuated dyemaker presided over a similar anachronism; he 'struck' dyes laboriously in a collection of antiquated ovens when they could, of course, have been bought outside at a fraction of the cost.

Shortly before Mr Gronow joined De La Rue as Stuart's managing director, Waterlow and Sons had bought up Waterlow Brothers and Leighton. Thus for a brief time Gronow was chief of the new Waterlow combine, and in this capacity had stumbled across the clandestine arrangement between Edgar Waterlow and Stuart de la Rue. The instant he arrived to take up his managing directorship in Bunhill Row he took his new chairman aside: now, he urged, that Waterlow and Sons owned Waterlow Brothers and Leighton, (who were still printing the English notes by photogravure) the Waterlow combine must honour Edgar Waterlow's secret agreement with Stuart, and recompense De La Rue with 6d for every thousand English notes they printed. (De La Rue, it may be remembered, had promised to pay Waterlows 1s a thousand if they printed the English notes by letterpress).

Surprised that he had not thought of the idea himself Stuart de la Rue was readily led to believe that Waterlows could be forced to pay some urgently needed cash into Bunhill Row. De La Rue consequently brought an action against them, which was not finally settled until 10th April 1923. The Company won the case and £120,000's worth of Waterlow compensation. But for an unexpected turn of events in Court, for once all would have ended satisfactorily for De La Rue. Having been praised for his cooperation, and fully confident of victory, Stuart was just about to leave the witness box when he looked across at the Waterlow people and made an appalling blunder. He really could not understand, he said, why Waterlows should have begrudged paying up for *their* side of the bargain over the English currency notes when

De La Rue had always honoured a similar promise to pay Waterlow for keeping out of their stamp monopoly.

Ears pricked at this revelation. The skeletons began tumbling out of the cupboard. It emerged that as far back as Sir Thomas Andros's time there had been a private agreement between the head of De La Rue and the head of Waterlow: De La Rue were to have home and colonial territory and Waterlows the foreign market. If by mistake a De La Rue tender for foreign stamps was accepted, compensation was duly made to Waterlow, Sir Thomas Andros invariably entrusting his youngest son, Stuart, with the task of carrying round the money in a black Gladstone bag from Bunhill Row to Great Winchester Street, where he placed it in the hands of Edgar Waterlow himself. The rest of the Waterlow family knew nothing of this arrangement.

Not only was the printing world aghast, but also His Majesty's Government. Stuart de la Rue's unthinking admission sent shock waves through the departments involved. The Crown Agents, the Foreign Office, the Treasury all clamoured for an inquiry. When one was set up, Stuart received a public admonishment, and was fortunate that no stronger action was taken against him.

With his back against the wall Stuart made a last desperate move. He invited the staff of Bunhill Row to his office, one after the other, and requested them to state what they felt was wrong with the Company. Even Bernard Westall, the junior clerk, was asked; he had nothing to lose by speaking out: 'You', he said to Stuart de la Rue.

The effect on his chairman may be imagined. Stuart spluttered to his Board that either 'that whippersnapper Westall' went, or he did. At that time the only other members of the Board consisted of two outside business investors who had been observing Stuart's antics with increasing concern. The view expressed by young Westall echoed their own thoughts. They accepted Stuart's ultimatum; only to his incredulous fury it was he who went and Westall whom they kept.

---

# CHAPTER XIX

# Sidney Lamert:
# new architect, old problems

With the exit of Stuart there were no de la Rues left in the firm. After the disgrace of the public inquiry Gronow was also dismissed, and the firm was virtually leaderless. To bridge the gap the Board persuaded a Scotsman called Sidney Lamert to be chairman and managing director.

He was the son of an irascible Scottish parson. Like a famous contemporary he went out to South Africa as a war correspondent, but unlike Churchill managed to avoid being taken prisoner by the Boers. On his return he bought with his accumulated savings a substantial interest in an unimportant weekly called the *Investors Chronicle*. It was a lucky buy. The rubber boom arose, stimulating public interest in the Stock Market. The circulation of his paper soared and his fortune was made. Mr Lamert's name began to be mentioned in City circles.

His immediate challenge in De La Rue was to face the debenture holders, who amongst other things had financed the take-over of the Goodall Playing Card Company. Because Stuart de la Rue had allowed a duplication of effort to persist, with the Goodall plant continuing to operate in Camden Town and the De La Rue one in Bunhill Row, this purchase had in no way boosted profits. Mr Lamert found nothing encouraging to report about playing cards, or indeed anything else.

When he launched the debenture issue in 1921, Stuart de la Rue had fixed the interest payable to its investors at the unusually high rate of 8 per cent. There was never the slightest hope of being able to pay it. Mr Lamert told the debenture holders that the Company's assets would not even cover De La Rue's trade debts, and nor were they themselves at the head of the debenture queue. After the loss of the Inland Revenue order in 1911, the de la Rue brothers had issued a first lot of debentures. There would not be a penny left for the second debenture holders.

The latter received this news with profound dissatisfaction. When it was suggested that the one pound shares be reduced in value to sixpence, and that fifty ordinary shares be accepted for every debenture, they remained unmollified. The announcement that there was no hope of a dividend in the foreseeable future scarcely helped, and the meeting disrupted into a storm of recrimination against Stuart de la Rue's erstwhile mismanagement. Sidney Lamert stood his ground. He pointed out that the debenture holders had no alternative but to accept his proposals, and his resoluteness won the day.

\*　　　\*　　　\*

Mr Lamert then started looking into the Company's assets. He uncovered an extraordinary state of affairs. Machines bought fifty or sixty years ago figured in the accounts at their original purchase prices. Shortly before his departure Stuart de la Rue had all this machinery valued and, considering it to be family property, sold it back to the Company. Solicitors' letters were sent to Stuart demanding substantial reparation. After some haggling he eventually offered to pay back the paltry sum of £30,000. Unwilling to run the risk of a long law suit, Sidney Lamert accepted it.

Against all odds a De La Rue break through occurred at this critical moment. Sidney Lamert did not believe in the new copper plate methods of printing. In fact he did not believe the firm had a future of any kind in security printing. He thought that the Company should be concentrating on stationery, in effect reverting to the early days of Thomas the founder.

At this juncture Bernard Westall requested Mr Lamert's permission to look round for another position. The Chairman agreed, adding sympathetically that he thought Westall was right to do so since he himself saw no future for De La Rue.

But by a strange coincidence a letter arrived the next day from the Government of Siam, announcing its intention to have a new currency issue. It wished to change over from letterpress to copperplate printing and accordingly invited De La Rue to send a representative to Bangkok. Mr Lamert was in a quandary. The Company had been printing the Siamese notes by letterpress for the last twenty years. He was loath to lose one of the few remaining orders De La Rue had. Yet holding no faith in the future of either banknote printing or copperplate, he had not encouraged the development of the rotary copperplate machine. Even the cost of transporting a representative to Bangkok was daunting. Doubtfully he asked Westall if he would care to go. The latter jumped at the chance. Again he had nothing to lose, and the excursion postponed the immediate necessity of finding another post.

Twenty-nine year old Bernard Westall found himself in a four berth cabin aboard a P. and O. ship sailing to places he had only read about and never expected to see: the Suez Canal, Aden, Bombay, Colombo. Like Lamert he was the son of a parson, a particularly impecunious one, the intensity of the Rev. Arthur St Ledger Westall's beliefs having led him from the Church of England to the Church of Rome, and back again. As Father Westall was descended from a long line of clerics with large families and small stipends, he had little money of his own. Scholarships enabled his eldest son Bernard to go from grammar school to Cambridge, where he read Classics like his father, with the similar intention of entering the Church. He took a wartime degree before going out with the Essex regiment to France, and later Gallipoli. He thought his foreign travels had ended there.

With fifty pounds in his pocket, which was supposed to last for three months, he disembarked at Penang, caught the weekly train from Prai on the mainland, chugged through rubber plantation and jungle, and arrived in Bangkok. There, on the banks of the Menam, the mosquitoes were so powerful that in the evenings visitors were handed a sarong in which to enshroud their legs. Westall got into his first rickshaw and proceeded unceremoniously to the compound of the Royal Palace, where the Ministry of Finance is situated. He saw the Government's British adviser, who dashed any hopes by stating crisply that he had warned the Siamese against dealing with De La Rue.

When Westall eventually obtained an interview with the Controller General, Phya Anaraks Kosa, news of the firm's financial precariousness had preceded him. Why, Phya Anaraks wanted to know, should his Government do business with a company which was liable to go bankrupt at any moment? There was only one answer. Frankly, said Westall, De La Rue needed the order more than any of the other firms and could therefore be relied upon to put in a very low price. He suggested that a clause could be inserted into a contract with De La Rue, stipulating that if the worst happened, and the Company went into liquidation, the plates and paper remained the property of the Siamese Government and could be handed over to one of the other printers. Still nervous about the Company's future, Phya Anaraks was nevertheless attracted by the notion that if De La Rue were allowed to tender everyone else would have to trim their prices.

The solitary question that remained was the fact that the Siamese required copperplate printing in which De La Rue were known to be inexperienced. That problem, countered Westall, was easily disposed of; would the Government be prepared to have Waterlow, the acknowledged copperplate experts, print the new issue? 'Of course', answered the Controller General. 'Well then', he rejoined, '*a fortiori* you should be satisfied with De La Rue.

Perhaps you are unaware that leading personnel in Waterlow have recently transferred to De La Rue?' Agreeably surprised the Controller General began to soften and granted Westall permission to tender.

Although the first Siamese hurdle was crossed, others lay ahead. When Westall was handed a copy of the specification an immediate difficulty beset him – he had no idea what price he should offer. De La Rue affairs were still so haphazard that Bunhill Row possessed no estimating department. He spent an anxious night in his hot hotel bedroom trying to calculate the potential output of the unfinished rotary copperplate machine, plus overheads, the percentage of wastage and the cost of subsequent operations. That done he borrowed the hotel typewriter, with one finger tapped out his calculations, and took his offer round to Phya Anaraks Kosa the next morning.

It was a week before anything happened. Idling meanwhile over the pages of the *Bangkok Times*, Westall read that the Siamese Government was experiencing some difficulty with forged customs certificates. He presented himself at the Customs office. The junior official he saw was a contemporary of his at Cambridge, who was called Prince Viwat. In a city of many princes he was destined to become a world figure, not only Minister of Finance and an authority at the World Bank, but also the statesman who headed his country's deputation at the Kandy peace treaty conference after World War II.

Prince Viwat was struck by Westall's idea of introducing a security device into customs forms. He persuaded his chief to order some from De La Rue. The little plastics factory in Walthamstow profited too. Insulators were about the only product it was capable of making, and Westall sold a quantity to the Siamese Post Office for telephone poles.

During the enforced wait he was getting acutely short of money. Luckily for him he was an exceptionally good bridge player and was able to supplement his finances. Phya Anaraks eventually lifted his spirits by sending for him again. Only one thing prevented him from giving De La Rue the contract, he confided; how would he know that De La Rue, having quoted a low price, would not be tempted to put it up after completing the first order? 'By multiplying the quantities of notes to be ordered by five, and stipulating delivery over five years', suggested Westall. Phya Anaraks capitulated and gave De La Rue a five year contract.

Westall's nocturnal mental arithmetic proved to be accurate. His estimated figure was within a couple of hundred pounds of the actual cost of the £125,000 order. To Mr Lamert's amazement the Siamese visit had been a resounding success. As a result of it Portals, the papermakers, received a letter from their agents which began: 'De La Rue have a Banknote enquiry for us *at last* . . .' The sentiment was shared to a heartfelt degree by everyone at Bunhill Row.

# CHAPTER XX

## *Effects of demolition*

One of Stuart de la Rue's biggest lapses had been his failure to maintain the lead held by the Onoto pen. Its fame lingered until after 1918. Field Marshal Haig used his throughout the war, and vouchsafed appreciatively: 'It never failed me'. But by the time Mr Lamert arrived on the scene in 1923 a vigorous effort was necessary in order to resuscitate it. Precious money was again expended on its advertisement.

Trade journals were induced to carry Onoto 'testimonials', the improbability of which was occasionally staggering. 'F.J.B.' wrote from H.M.S. *Caradoc*: 'I have had it about 5 years during which time I have dropped it dozens of times and none too gently. Several times I have dropped it on the nib which I have straightened with a hammer, and it has always come up smiling. It was originally a medium nib, and having a desire to obtain a fine nib I tried filing it, but the metal tip proved too good, so eventually I put it on an emery wheel'. Another man wrote in to say that while working in his garden he dug up an Onoto which had been buried for four and a half years. After cleaning it, he removed the cap from the pen and out of curiosity turned on the valve '. . . the pen wrote perfectly with a clear appearance of fresh ink'.

The stationers were impressed by these miracles and the Onoto inched its way back into the public eye. Edgar Wallace eulogised it, Dorothy Sayers used it as a clue, and De La Rue ink was celebrated in the music halls, where such jokes were perpetrated as: 'The Princess's blood is so blue that Onoto wants the recipe'.

In the midst of this newfound success Mr Lamert decided to move the pen factory up to Scotland. Speaking *ex tempore*, for he had the disarming habit of addressing annual general meetings as though they were after-dinner gatherings, he divulged to his shareholders that he had been having union troubles. He had therefore acquired a factory in Fife, beyond the union's reach. Those Bunhill Row pen hands who did not favour moving north had been discharged, and new ones found to replace them. What Mr Lamert did not realize was that one of the dismissed pen hands was present at the meeting as a shareholder. Within a couple of days the union organizer was up at Strathendry, and within a month all new hands were back in the same old union. It was like the man who ran away to Samarra to escape Death, and found she had made an appointment to meet him there. The Onoto might just as well have stayed put because it died from its transplanting.

\*　　\*　　\*

When Thomas de la Rue faced his 1837 crisis his firm's decline in fortunes coincided with national economic disasters. The same pattern was recurring in the 1920s. The general strike and the depression exacerbated the Company's already critical condition. At a Mansion House banquet given in February 1926 to mark the opening of the British Industries Fair, the Prince of Wales with more feeling than eloquence lamented: 'We have had a bad time, a very bad time, and there are still some who are having a bad time'.

When King George V visited the fair at the White City he was enraged to learn that the typewriters used in his Government's offices were of American origin. 'It is scandalous!' he cried. Still fuming he continued his tour, pausing at the De La Rue stand to look at some new plastics: 'All made of milk, m'dear', he explained inaccurately to Queen Mary. 'Aren't they?' he barked crossly at Sidney Lamert, hovering nervously by. We cannot but sympathize with the Chairman in his dilemma. 'Yes Sir', replied Sidney untruthfully.

In its house journal, the *Pillar Box*, De La Rue loyally echoed the Sovereign's sentiments about 'Buying British'. Beneath a picture of the Union Jack the editor banged his drum in an article called 'Follow the Flag': 'We live in days of far away development and enterprise, days of all red routes . . . when it is an absolute necessity for our Great Manufacturing Houses to be up and doing, to be keenly alive to the mutual benefits occurring from a great inter-Empire trade, strengthening the kindly bonds which unite the Old Country and its Children beyond the Seas'. The *Pillar Box*'s editor reported with pride that the Company had responded to the challenge. 'The House of De La Rue being fully cognisant of the necessities of the situation, have dispatched abroad their export manager, Mr John Tredwen'. There was a photograph of Mr Tredwen posed nonchalantly in flannels beside the Pyramids. But success eluded him, and apart from a spell or two of dysentery he had nothing to report.

# CHAPTER XXI

## *Out of the rubble*

After another trip to Bangkok in 1928 Bernard Westall became assistant managing director to Sidney Lamert. He thus became senior to his father-in-law, Mr Rapkin, who did not greet the development with enthusiasm.

De La Rue had just won a contract for printing bonds for the Government of Spain which laid special emphasis on security measures. It was unfortunate, to say the least, that Mr Rapkin should choose this moment to experiment with copper electros and to select the Spanish bond plate for his touchstone. To his horror Bernard discovered that, strictly against the terms of the contract, his father-in-law had ordered half a dozen electros to be made from the original.

De La Rue seemed doomed to yet another generation of family quarrels. Mr Westall had no option but to inform the rest of the Board that as long as his father-in-law remained a director, with power to intervene in printing matters, the Company's chances of recovery were negligible. The Board agreed with him, and he went tactfully off to Dublin while Sidney Lamert undertook the delicate task of persuading Mr Rapkin to resign. Halfway through he got stuck, and wired for Westall to come back and clarify the situation to his father-in-law, who was being slow to take the point.

On his return Westall made the point very clearly indeed. Rapkin brought his solicitor to their subsequent meetings and refused to speak to him. Each addressed the solicitor as if he were an interpreter. Temporarily the position was a difficult one for

Mrs Westall who was belaboured by her father's friends and relations until she felt like the Elephant's Child. But the upset did not last long.

As Mr Lamert was busy with his other interests, Bernard Westall was virtually vice-chairman, managing director and works manager rolled into one, liable to be in Athens or Ankara or Madrid or Sofia, or wherever there was a chance of getting some printing business. In the early nineteen twenties, had someone entertained the idea of buying up De La Rue with its one pound shares standing at half-a-crown, a mere £80,000 would have sufficed to clinch the deal. Now, after the arrival of Mr Westall in the board room, the sum needed for any such transaction began to rise. What qualities of brilliance enabled him to breathe back life into an organization so nearly defunct that its heartbeat was inaudible?

In many ways he resembled the mercurial character of the first Thomas de la Rue. Both worked intuitively rather than according to carefully laid plans, opportunists in the sense that they pounced on the chance of the moment and were prepared to gamble on it; visionaries in the sense that they could clearly envisage where their Company's future lay, and work towards it with single-minded gusto. That was their genius. They throve in the teeth of adversity, relished a challenge, and had the same restless energy. Neither suffered fools gladly, though whereas Thomas's wrath sometimes never dispersed at all, Bernard Westall's melted quickly. There was also something of Colonel Billy de la Rue in his make-up; they shared not only the born optimist's ability to charm and to sell, but a fundamental interest in people. They were what Italians term *simpatico*. Resembling Anthony Eden in appearance, to look at Bernard represented the foreigner's idea of a conventional Englishman. But having met him, Americans, for instance, could not believe he was English, and Continentals thought he might be American. Imaginative, ebullient, extrovert, he was quick to react to the prevailing mood, and was as capable of enfolding a Spaniard in a warm embrace as of inscrutably outwitting oriental opponents in an all-night sitting of mah-jong.

It is not altogether surprising that we find him taking the next unorthodox step of employing two foreigners to help with his sales work, two controversial ones at that. One was named Albert Avramow, and the other Peter Loopuyt. Loopuyt called on Mr Westall to sell him advertising space in the *Lady*. De La Rue did not buy any, but took Peter Loopuyt instead – and amongst some forty other periodicals later printed the *Lady*. Loopuyt was a debonair Dutchman who wore a monocle and was always being told by his numerous female admirers that he looked like a movie star called Conrad Veidt. He had been taken on by Lord Northcliffe after sending him an article called 'How I dined with the Kaiser' (in a railway train as it transpired). He got De La Rue a printing order from Latvia, and then entrenched himself in Spain, where he helped the Company win extensive banknote orders.

The other foreign salesman, Albert Avramow, was an equally improbable character for an old-established English company to employ. An excitable Bulgarian Jew, of Turkish origin, he was an unusual looking man with a low forehead, dark bushy eyebrows, and piercing eyes.

His most impressive achievement to date was his triumph for the American Banknote Company over Waterlow in Bulgaria in spite of his price being £50,000 higher. On that occasion he chanced to be sitting opposite an Englishman in the dining-car of the Simplon-Orient Express. Never shy, ever curious, Avramow asked him why he was travelling to Bulgaria. He turned out to be the American Bank Note Company's European manager and explained that he was going to try for the Bulgarian contract. 'You're the luckiest man on earth!' cried Avramow. 'You are sitting opposite the one man who can get you that contract. The Minister of Finance is a personal friend of mine'. By the time the train reached Sofia he had become the American Bank Note Company's agent in Bulgaria.

Having stipulated that the commission, including a handsome present for his friend the Minister, should be paid in advance, Avramow kept his promise. The American Bank Note Company got the order. Then some weeks later, glimpsing the police approaching his front door, he snatched up a suitcase bulging with his commission, escaped through the back door and caught the Simplon Express to Bucharest. His friend the Minister was less fortunate. He was tried for corruption and hanged. Avramow was never able to return to Bulgaria.

He always moved in an atmosphere of melodrama with comic opera overtones. Still carrying his bulging suitcase he left Bucharest for Paris, where he intended to get in touch with a firm of French leather manufacturers – a distant cousin in Bucharest having informed him that the Rumanians needed a large supply of army boots. But *en route* he collected an *amour* who wanted to go to Monte Carlo. He complied, lost the contents of his suitcase gambling with her at the Casino, just managed to return to Paris, borrowed the money for a single fare to England from a lady typist in the office of the American Bank Note Company and, armed with a glowing introduction from its benevolent manager to Waterlows and De La Rue, set off for London. He spent his last money on a shave, went to De La Rue first because it was nearer, and arrived in Mr Westall's office.

In retrospect Bernard Westall admits to some astonishment that he ever engaged so controversial a character. Mr Lamert, more cautious and conservative, took an instant dislike to him. Nonetheless Avramow had already proved he could get banknote business – and that was what was undeniably needed. Moreover Mr Westall had a shrewd idea that his forcefulness could be used in the new theatre of operations he had in mind for the firm – China.

# CHAPTER XXII

## *Reconstruction*

Before sending Avramow out East it was felt advisable to test him on a small mission nearer home. The country suggested was Italy, where no harm could be done since she already printed her own notes. In his broken English he enthusiastically bombarded Bunhill Row for Roman introductions.

Actually only one letter came to be written on his behalf – only one proved to be necessary. It was to Mussolini from Mr Westall. On the spur of the moment, without seriously thinking that there would be any reply, he wrote direct to Il Duce, reminding him that after helping a unified Italy to establish its postal and currency requirements, the brothers Warren and William Frederick de la Rue were decorated by King Victor Emmanuel on Cavour's recommendation. He wondered if the Duce would care to re-equip the State printing works with up-to-date presses. To everyone's amazement back came a letter from Mussolini expressing interest in the De La Rue proposal, and requesting the Company to send someone to Rome to discuss it. Avramow's task was therefore half completed for him before he arrived.

Although the Italian visit was not a real test of his capabilities Mr Westall was impressed by his enthusiasm and resolved to chance sending him to Chungking. He was more than ever convinced that China should be the Company's next target. Through sheer size of population her printing needs were enormous.

Confirming this theory a Chinese inquiry for four thousand

million postage stamps came in almost at once. Avramow won it at a good price. He cabled asking the Company to accept payment in American dollars. A firm believer in the everlasting value of the pound sterling, Westall mistakenly replied that he would prefer to be paid in sterling and would only accept dollars if the conditions of contract left no alternative. The Chinese Government possessed dollars but few pounds, and therefore insisted on paying in dollars. Avramow agreed. Before printing was started, the pound was devalued from 4.86 dollars to the pound to 4 dollars. Overnight De La Rue's price was consequently increased by 18 per cent. The last laugh was Avramow's.

\* \* \*

In the early thirties the house of De La Rue needed so many repairs that it was difficult to know where to start. For one thing, something had to be done about the plastics business. Originally the property of two Germans it had been appropriated during the first world war by the Disposal of Enemy Property Board, and bought at a cut price by Stuart de la Rue who never did anything to improve it. It still consisted of two small houses in Walthamstow, and an adjoining garden shed which was 'the factory'. Its best customer was a certain Allen Clark, whose American father owned a button-making business in Birmingham. Father and son invested in a minute engineering project, little more than a garage, which they bought from a man called Plessey in Ilford. There they made electric appliances, buying their plastic parts from the De La Rue shed in Walthamstow.

But it was all very small beer. If De La Rue plastics were to live they must be expanded. Greatly daring, the Company bought a ten-acre site in Avenue Road, Walthamstow, with permission to build a proper factory. Lowly orders for toothmugs and jelly cups trickled in. A visit to Oxford produced a few requests for window frames by Morris Motors, and later the frames were made on a bigger scale for Fords. When Plesseys got their first orders from the Post Office for telephones, each telephone they supplied meant seven mouldings for De La Rue.

The chronic ill-health of De La Rue playing card sales persisted. It was the time when the big tobacco companies were wooing the public with free gifts. Wills, of Imperial Tobacco, tucked two miniature cards into every packet of ten *Goldflake* or *Capstan*, and each complete set of miniatures posted to Wills's Bristol establishment entitled the sender to a pack of normal sized cards. The scheme caught on like a forest fire, and John Waddington of Leeds, the makers of these cards, revelled in it, to the discomfort of De La Rue. The latter did not find their contract with the makers of *Kensitas* to supply five gift coupons for every packet of cigarettes nearly so interesting. The coupons were convertible into tea sets and alarm clocks, not playing cards. John Waddington became swamped by the Wills demands, De La Rue helped out by making cards for Waddingtons, and eventually the tobacco companies came to their senses and abandoned their gift schemes. By this time saturation point had been reached. There was such a glut of playing cards that during the next two years public demand for them was nearly halved. Even so, an amicable arrangement having been made with Waddington, the firm's playing card profits at last began to pick up.

\*     \*     \*

In 1932, when Mr Westall as vice-chairman took control of the Company in Mr Lamert's absence abroad, he looked about for an idea to steady its shaky public image. It was essential to restore the confidence of foreign governments. Never again could foreign Finance Ministers be allowed to doubt the Company's powers of survival. Some way must be found of emphasizing the firm's venerable past. Bernard Westall asked the Company Secretary to find out what events were happening in Bunhill Row a century before. In 1832, as we know, Thomas took out his patent for 'Improvements to Playing Cards'. In 1932 Bernard considered this an adequate reason for an anniversary party and invited a handful of notables to dinner at the Savoy. There were two ambassadors, a couple of judges, the Minister of Labour, Mr R. H. Hudson and Gordon Selfridge, who proposed the Company's health. The next morning *The Times* gave De La Rue not only a column but a leader.

The De La Rue dinner became an annual fixture. Paradoxically as it got bigger it became a more private function. At the Company's request it was no longer reported in the Press. The Court of St James gradually came to attend *en masse*, together with so many figures from public life that over the years minor incidents inevitably occurred. In themselves these represent a small history of the times. Once the ambassadors of all the Arab States treated the De La Rue dinner like a United Nations Assembly, and walked out just before the Israeli Ambassador, the senior member of the diplomatic corps present, was due to make a speech.

On another occasion Sir Anthony Eden saved the situation when the Lord Chancellor, Lord Jowitt, felt he had been snubbed. Mr Attlee's Government had the slenderest majority and an important parliamentary debate on the same night necessitated the fullest attendance by Government members. The Minister of Labour, Alfred (now Lord) Robens, was forced to send a last minute note asking to be excused from speaking at the dinner – for just one absentee might bring about the fall of the Government. In referring to the reason for the Minister's absence, Westall could not resist adding: 'There must be many here tonight who much regret that Mr Robens is not with us at this moment'. Amid the laughter Lord Jowitt half rose from his seat to leave, but Sir Anthony pushed him back and told him not to be a bloody fool. The Lord Chancellor acquiesced; the next day he wrote to say how much he had enjoyed the evening and that he hoped he would be asked again next year.

During one of the wartime dinners at the Dorchester the sirens sounded. Ernest Bonn, the manager of the hotel, sent Bernard Westall a note saying: 'Air raid on. Nothing overhead'. Taking this to mean that there were no planes in the vicinity, Westall allowed the dinner to continue. Not until afterwards was the awful truth revealed. What Mr Bonn had tried to indicate was that there was nothing overhead except a glass roof. Since all three heads of the Armed Services were amongst the guests present, the full import of the misunderstanding was spine-chilling. The De La Rue directors thanked their stars that on that particular night, in June 1944, the Germans dropped their bombs on the other side of the Park.

*    *    *

The chief obstacle to a return to prosperity in the early thirties was the continued heavy rise in overheads. The situation had to be faced, and in 1932 an extraordinary general meeting was held at which it was proposed to write down the Company's shares, reducing its capital by sixty per cent. The holder of a hundred shares would become the proprietor of forty. Largely because he was able to convince the shareholders that the near future held promise, particularly in China, the Managing Director had surprisingly little trouble. It was thus possible to write off the obsolete plant in Bunhill Row and to re-value the buildings at a realistic figure. The unabsorbed overheads disappeared and in 1933 De La Rue made a trading profit for the first time in twenty years.

Morale in Bunhill Row, which had sunk as low as the Company's fortunes, began to revive. The next decade of the thirties is remembered by De La Rue people as being the most exciting time in their careers. They heard the small but unmistakable sound of a business beginning to hum again.

# CHAPTER XXIII

## *Chinese Pavilion*

Sidney Lamert was touring abroad in 1933 and 1934. On his return Bernard Westall went to meet him at Croydon Airport. With his first breath Lamert called for Albert Avramow's instant dismissal, and in the car on the way to London backed up his demand by producing photographs of letters he had written to Westall from the East and given to Avramow to post. Anxious to know what his visiting chairman was saying about him, which as he suspected was far from complimentary, Avramow had been consistently steaming open the envelopes and getting a Chinese clerk in his Shanghai office to photograph the contents. Scenting the possibility of making a few dollars, the Chinese clerk carefully preserved the negatives and sold copies of all the Chairman's letters back to the latter before he left for England.

The revelation of the seamier side of Avramow's character came as no shock to Mr Westall. Mr Lamert, on the other hand, could not pardon such ungentlemanly behaviour. Westall countered that De La Rue were not out in China to set standards of behaviour but to get orders. They settled on a compromise. Avramow was to be rusticated for a period but not sent down.

When next he presented himself in London Albert Avramow gleefully brought back with him an order for a couple of million notes from the Chinese Bank of Communications. Nonetheless the promise to Mr Lamert was honoured, and for the time being he was kept on a short European leash. Another representative, who was sent out to take his place, transmitted news of the mouthwatering orders to be had from the big Chinese banks. Yet none of them seemed to be coming the Company's way. Despite fierce opposition from the Chairman, who resigned in protest from the joint managing directorship, Westall set Avramow free. On his return to the East he justified his liberation by obtaining business from the Farmer's Bank, and from the Bank of China in Tientsin.

In the beginning the delivery of the Bank of China's notes was hazardous. The very first shipment ran into trouble between Shanghai and Tientsin. The ship was seized by pirates, who sailed it down to an island in the China seas where they landed the passengers, all nuns on their way to a Mission. The story caught the eye of the world's press but ended happily for everyone. The nuns were duly rescued, thinner, though no worse for their adventure, and De La Rue emerged unscathed – their banknotes, being the first of a series of designs, were not yet in circulation. In any case Bunhill Row had insured against such contingencies and it remained only to print another series of notes in a different colour.

A new Chinese bank, the Central Bank, was being formed with Dr H. H. Kung, the Minister of Finance, as Governor. Together with his brother-in-law, T.V. Soong, he ranked next in China's governmental hierarchy to Generalissimo Chiang Kai-shek, who was also his brother-in-law. The wives of these men were even more remarkable than their husbands, their third sister was the widow of Dr Sun Yat-sen, acclaimed as founder of modern China. Graced with rare intelligence and beauty, the sisters were known as 'The Three Bamboos'.

Albert Avramow cabled Bunhill Row that Dr H. H. Kung's new bank would have extensive requirements and that tenders were being invited for the printing of all its banknotes. The matter was too big for him to handle. Would Mr Westall come out and help? He replied that he was too busy.

Without any warning Avramow turned up at Croydon airport. Like an excited dog panting to take its master for a walk he rushed

A. G. Norman, aged 21

Dr H. H. Kung,
Chinese Minister of Finance

Bernard Westall in an air-raid shelter in
Chungking

14. Bunhill Row early in the nineteenth century

After the Blitz

into Bunhill Row to repeat his request. From his torrent of talk one fact became clear: the new bank's inquiry was for ninety million notes, each with three copperplate printings ... Mr Westall and Avramow left for China immediately.

As soon as they arrived in Chungking they went round to see Dr Kung. The Minister of Finance was a short, plump, bespectacled person with a little military moustache and a manner so frigidly formal as to make Westall suspect some previous maladroitness on Albert's part. The next morning he left him behind and went back to see the Minister alone. After a few delicate preliminaries Dr Kung unburdened himself of the tale of the jade necklace.

Hoping to win over one of the Three Bamboos as an ally, Albert had gone to some pains to discover the day of Madame Kung's birthday, which that year was on a Sunday. She was a devout Christian. He waited outside the church which she regularly attended, and as she left presented her with a valuable jade necklace. Drawing himself up as high as his stature permitted Dr Kung handed this necklace to Bernard Westall with a pair of sugar tongs. He expatiated on the extent of Avramow's insult to his wife and to himself, regretting that however far Mr Westall might have travelled to see him the idea of doing business with Albert Avramow's Company was totally distasteful.

Unprepared for this development Bernard Westall thought fast. Avramow being Jewish, he pointed out, was himself accustomed to a semi-oriental way of doing business. Had it not been the custom for the last five thousand years for the great leaders of China to accept presents as their right? How was Avramow to know that after so many centuries China at last possessed a Finance Minister of impeccable integrity? Dr Kung conceded that there could conceivably have been a misunderstanding. He would allow De La Rue to have part of the order after all. In fact he would give the American Bank Note Company, Waterlow and De La Rue a third each.

Not unnaturally the American Bank Note Company fought hard to prevent De La Rue from achieving this success. Dr Kung sent for Mr Westall and inquired anxiously about the Company's delivery dates. The American Bank Note Company had advised him that De La Rue, who possessed only a small plant and were just beginning to re-emerge as banknote printers, could not hope to complete the order on time. He asked apprehensively whether the Company would agree to a penalty clause of a hundred pounds a day if they got behind with their deliveries. Westall replied that if Dr Kung would increase the penalty clause to a thousand pounds a day, De La Rue would be glad to accept the condition. The Minister's doubts dispersed.

As a parting present Dr Kung gave De La Rue an additional order for 60 million notes accompanied by the request that all future negotiations be conducted exclusively between himself and Mr Westall – this condition would entail some intensive travelling for the latter but he could hardly refuse.

*     *     *

When the news of the Chinese banknote orders reached the Board room at Bunhill Row it was not welcomed. Mr Westall received a letter from Mr Lamert deploring the volume of Chinese business which had been accepted, and complaining that the Company had not the capacity to execute it. Once back in London he arranged with the suppliers of copperplate equipment, Brotherhoods of Peterborough, that De La Rue would double the price for their castings if they could be delivered to Bunhill Row in a third of the usual time.

Brotherhoods kept their promise; to keep theirs De La Rue had a hair-raising race against time. The week before delivery was due the excitement in Bunhill Row was at fever pitch. The actual printing was done but there were only five days left for cutting, examining, counting and packing. The girls in the banknote finishing department responded bravely and would have worked all night, but it was against the law. Instead every male in the office staff worked round the clock under the management of Ernest Gough. The notes were completed by dawn on the Friday, packed, crated and sent to the Port of London whence they all sailed for China punctually on the Saturday.

Recalling the drama, people from Bunhill Row say they found something irresistible about it which made them eager for similar challenges. Daily chores shed their monotony, everyone felt they mattered. When the girls in the Finishing Department arrived on the final morning they found improbable people, including all executive directors, scurrying about unshaven in shirtsleeves doing unlikely jobs in an end-of-term atmosphere. There was a sense of almost wartime urgency.

The herculean labours in London EC1 did not pass unnoticed by Dr Kung in Shanghai. He summoned Bernard Westall to discuss further plans. On the way out, the ship stayed two nights in port at Singapore. Bernard went to Raffles Hotel where a New Zealand reporter from the *Straits Times* sought an interview to ask the purpose of his visit. In his answer Bernard made a bad blunder. He talked about banknotes in general and added that R.M.S. *Carthage*, the ship in which he was travelling, happened by coincidence to be carrying a few million De La Rue notes to the Chinese Bank of Communications. The next morning he was dismayed to find a banner headline across the front page of the *Straits Times:* 'MILLIONS OF BANKNOTES FOR CHINA'.

His apprehension was well founded. He had no sooner arrived in Shanghai than Dr Kung summoned him peremptorily to his office and threw across his desk a copy of the South China Daily News. The *Straits Times* story was reproduced in full. Dr Kung was beside himself with fury. 'You have told the whole world we are inflating', he shouted. 'It's up to you to put the damage right'. Bernard caught the one daily four-seater plane to Hong Kong to see the editor of the *South China Daily News*, told him of his difficulty

THE HOUSE THAT THOMAS BUILT

with the Chinese Minister of Finance, and asked him to print a correction. He refused. But he agreed instead to print a dissertation by Bernard about Chinese banknotes, mentioning the De La Rue order, emphasizing that its purpose was to replace old soiled notes, and stating that it was the firm intention of H.E. Dr Kung to protect the Chinese people from the danger of unhygenic, easily forged ones.

With a copy of the morning paper containing the article in his brief case Westall flew back to Shanghai. Dr Kung read it and shook his hand vigorously. Relieved that a disaster for his Ministry had been averted, Dr Kung was disposed to appreciate that a major mistake had been transformed into something agreeably complimentary to all concerned. Much giving and receiving of congratulatory dinners followed.

*     *     *

Air-travel in China was still in its infancy. Yet time was short and the area of business to be covered huge. Mr Westall and Avramow flew up to Hankow in a plane of uncertain temperament to visit the Governor of the Farmer's Bank. They followed the route of the Yangste some thousand miles up river, catching alarming glimpses of the snow-covered Chinese hills beneath them through a crack in the floor.

China's currency was divided into two categories, the yuan or 'big money', and the cent or 'little money'. The three issuing banks (other than the Central or Government Bank) had to seek permission from the Minister of Finance before they could print their own yuan notes. The Governor of the Farmer's Bank had been refused permission to print 50 million yuan notes. He then conceived the bright idea of issuing a fifty cent note, which being 'little money' did not require Dr Kung's approval. By reducing the size and number of printings he was able to get a hundred million fifty cent notes (half a yuan) for the price of 50 million one yuan notes. Honour was satisfied all round.

Even so Dr Hsiu, the Governor of the Farmer's Bank, could not refrain from bargaining. An argument about delivery dates ensued. Bernard Westall remained adamant: the first shipment would go out in four months. After weary hours the Governor agreed. The next morning Mr Westall and Avramow brought Dr Hsiu the contract to sign. He looked it through and promptly rescinded everything he had conceded the night before, put his feet up on the table and started reading a newspaper. Westall understood the Chinese mentality well enough by now to realise that it would be fatal for him to lose face. He removed Dr Hsiu's newspaper, told him that he had not flown a thousand miles in order to be insulted, and that rudeness was something he did not expect from a Chinese gentleman. If Dr Hsiu wished to negotiate with De La Rue he must do so through Avramow. He personally could have nothing more to do with him. Taking a leaf out of Dr Kung's book he thus handed back the argument with a pair of metaphorical sugar-tongs and stalked out of the room. Seeing the prospects of his commission disappearing in front of his eyes, Avramow ran after him almost in tears, pleading with Mr Westall to change his attitude. When they got back to their hotel a note from Dr Hsiu was already waiting for Avramow, asking him to go round and sign the contract and Dr Hsiu himself came to the airport to see them off.

On Mr Westall's next visit to Shanghai Dr Kung let fall that Generalissimo Chiang Kai-shek wished him to represent the Chinese Government at the Coronation of King George VI. Westall suggested that De La Rue could help with advance publicity so that the British people would know something about Dr Kung – he was, for instance, inordinately proud of his relationship to Kung Fu Tse (Confucius) whose seventy-fifth lineal descendant he claimed to be. The publicity idea pleased him very much. He accepted Bernard's offer and hinted that during his visit to England he would be discussing further orders for banknotes.

When Confucius's descendant eventually got into his Pullman at Dover he was gratified to see that the magazines and papers on the table carried his photograph on the front page. The next day he lunched at Bunhill Row, toured the works, and told De La Rue it was a great Company. Later he telephoned the Managing Director to say that if previous prices could be maintained he would give De La Rue banknote orders totalling some 800 millions to be divided over the four issuing banks.

Dazed by the amounts mentioned Mr Westall presented himself as requested in Dr Kung's Dorchester Hotel suite at eight o'clock the next morning. The Minister was having his breakfast. He looked up, glared at him, and crossly told him to sit down. In the ominous silence that followed Westall reflected on the volatile character of his customer, so different from his original conception of the inscrutable oriental. A second afterwards all hell broke loose. Dr Kung waved his arms about, upset his milk over his trousers and shouted that his General Manager had just telephoned from Shanghai. Dozens and dozens of faulty De La Rue notes had arrived: 'Wrong numbers. Incorrect quantity in certain packets. How can I trust you?' – adding dangerously: 'The American Bank Note Company *never* made a mistake'. Westall fetched a towel from the bathroom, mopped him up, and replied as soothingly as he could that it was bad for Dr Kung to get worked up; he should relax and finish his breakfast and they would talk about something else until he felt calmer.

By this time it was after nine o'clock, and Westall suggested that it might be helpful if Dr Kung had a word on the telephone with Mr S. B. Chamberlain, the Manager of the Bank of England's note printing establishments. Grudgingly Dr Kung telephoned Mr Chamberlain and asked him point blank whether the Bank of England ever made any mistakes in its note issues. Mr Chamberlain replied that so long as banknotes were printed, finished and examined by humans some mistakes would be inevitable.

Dr Kung put down the receiver with a smile and blandly remarked that the American Bank Note Company obviously did not employ humans. 'Could it be, Dr Kung', Mr Westall ventured to suggest, 'that somewhere in some department of your Central Bank, there might be someone who is all too human?' With the Minister's guffaws punctuating the rest of the proceedings their meeting ended with De La Rue receiving a contract to the value of nearly three million pounds, the biggest order in its history.

# CHAPTER XXIV

## *More than bricks and mortar*

Repeat orders were starting to pour in from all sides. In Madrid the widow of the Governor of the Bank of Spain, the Condessa de Sagasta, arranged for Peter Loopuyt to continue to do business with the Sub-Governor, Pedro Pan. Thereafter De La Rue printed all Spanish notes till the collapse of the Government forces in the Civil War. Señor Pan joined General Franco's side and, at the height of the struggle, telephoned Bunhill Row to say he had been appointed Governor of the new Bank of Spain, and as such was placing orders with De La Rue. These the Company reluctantly declined to accept. It could not become printers to two Banks of Spain, however tempting the offers might be.

In Bulgaria the firm observed at first hand some indications of the Nazi menace. The year was 1938. Mr Westall found himself assembled in Sofia with all the other major banknote printing representatives to compete for a new note issue. Their respective tenders were formally opened by the Governor, Dr Gunev, and read out in the presence of the Board of the Bank. Like examinees they were required to reassemble in the afternoon, when Dr Gunev announced that the order had gone to De La Rue.

That night in the Hotel Bulgaria, Dr Funk, the German Minister of Finance, was pointed out to Westall at the next table. He was told he had just arrived in Sofia to discuss the German purchase of the entire Bulgarian tobacco crop. He was therefore intrigued to see joining Dr Funk at his table none other than the representatives of the German Banknote Company, who had been amongst the unsuccessful competitors against De La Rue that afternoon. From snatches of conversation it was apparent that Dr Funk was about to see the Prime Minister.

The following morning Westall received an urgent note from the Governor of the Bank asking him to follow its bearer. In cloak and dagger fashion the messenger led him through devious side streets and back doors, all of which had to be unlocked, to the Governor's office. There, moved to tears, Dr Gunev told him that he had been forced to bow to his Prime Minister's insistence that the banknote order be given to the Germans. Unquestionably Dr Gunev had tried to resist the Nazi demands, for he himself was liquidated shortly afterwards.

The atmosphere in Sofia was becoming electric. The Munich crisis was imminent. One member of the Bulgarian Government was shot and killed outside his office and the city was put under martial law. Westall was not allowed to leave his hotel. Temporarily incarcerated, despondent at the Nazi seizure of the Bulgarian banknote order, even more depressed by the alarming deterioration of the international situation, he considered the position of De La Rue in the event of a world war. One thing was certain. With its factories concentrated in the environs of Bunhill Row the Company was in a desperately vulnerable position. What could be done at this eleventh hour to decentralize away from London? There was only one hopeful possibility.

Before Mr Westall left for Bulgaria it had come to De La Rue ears that Mr Howard Pillow, who was the major shareholder in the British-American Bank Note Company in Canada, was anxious to sell. This was exactly the chance the firm needed – an entry into the North American market, bringing with it Canadian, even American business. Better still it would offer an alternative production base, thereby avoiding over-concentration in Bunhill Row. Being a British company there would be no problem in transferring personnel to Montreal. When feelers were first put out to him on behalf of De La Rue Mr Pillow was pleased at the idea of his company remaining in British hands.

To set the financial wheels in motion, De La Rue consulted the merchant banking firm of Erlangers. Mr Kiek, a director of Erlangers, suggested that his own son, Peter, be dispatched immediately to Montreal to start inquiries. Having extracted himself from the gloom of Sofia, Westall found the post-Munich London scene equally cheerless. The one ray of light was an enthusiastic report from Montreal by Peter Kiek.

The Canadians were eager to meet Westall. He set out for Montreal accompanied by young Kiek and Sidney Lamert who was agog to see the outcome. The deal stood to represent the biggest single investment De La Rue had ever made. A warm welcome was waiting from Mr Pillow. After drinks at the Ritz Carlton he invited the English party to dinner with his wife and his daughter, Margaret. Margaret's husband, Murray Vaughan, was away on business. The evening went well. At the end of it Mr Pillow drew Westall cordially aside and said he would be happy to sell out at the price he had mentioned to Peter Kiek – £250,000. Equally successful was the subsequent meeting with the company's President, Charles Cowan. Matters were given into the hands of lawyers to settle, and by the week's end the formal sale should have awaited signature. But by Friday the legal ends were still not quite tied up. Everyone was assured that one more day would suffice.

On Saturday morning Howard Pillow asked the De La Rue delegation round to his office to toast the deal in champagne. But once more the lawyers telephoned apologetically to say they had been delayed. All would unquestionably be resolved by Monday; did the De La Rue party mind staying on? It did mind. Its bookings to New York and hence to London had to be cancelled. Yet, as there was no alternative, it reluctantly agreed to remain over the weekend. The two De La Rue directors played bridge and

Peter Kiek took Margaret Pillow Vaughan to the Governor General's Ball, the highlight of the social season.

The delay proved disastrous. Early on Sunday morning Bernard Westall was woken by an incoherent telephone call from Howard Pillow. Two facts emerged from his near-hysterical conversation; he was distraught about his daughter, Margaret, and the deal with De La Rue was off. Westall hurried round to his house and found him in a bad way. Peter Kiek wanted to elope with Margaret. Inclined to be hot tempered at the best of times, this development had sent Mr Pillow nearly berserk.

And so it came about that the plan to secure the future of De La Rue had perished because of a Governor General's Ball. Lamert and Westall returned empty-handed to Bunhill Row.

*    *    *

On the other side of the world, meanwhile, Japan was penetrating deep into the Chinese interior. The area was so vast, the population so teeming, that it was difficult for the intruders to keep control of the land through which they passed. It was as much as they could do to protect their forward troops and their lines of communication. In the districts where they were most powerful they set up a Nipponese directed Central Bank, and issued notes under its name.

As Chinese Minister of Finance Dr Kung was deeply concerned about maintaining the issue of the Chinese Yuan in these places; he was also apprehensive about the safety of Shanghai, whose international status Tokyo had hitherto respected. He approached a large American concern with an invitation to establish a banknote printing plant in the French concession in Shanghai. Fearing the city would soon be taken over by the Japanese, the Americans asked for certain guarantees. These were impossible to give, so instead Dr Kung wondered if De La Rue would be able to cope with the undertaking.

Once more Mr Westall and Avramow embarked for China.

With them they took a twenty-one year old recruit whom Bernard Westall thought would shoulder the exacting task of running the proposed Shanghai venture. His name was Gerry Norman. The son of a Somerset farmer Norman had joined the company straight from school on the recommendation of his house-master, Rupert Westall, a cousin of the Managing Director, who considered him to be one of the most promising pupils he had ever had. He is now Chairman of De La Rue.

Leaving young Norman temporarily in Hong Kong, Mr Westall and Avramow went to Hanoi, where they were to take the one remaining plane of the China National Air Company that had not been shot down by the Japanese. But the Managing Director caught malaria and Avramow proceeded to Chungking alone. However, Mr Westall's presence was insisted upon, and when he had more or less recovered a skilful American pilot, cloud hopping to avoid Japanese fighters, flew him via Kungming to Dr Kung. There was no European hotel left in Chungking, so Avramow had registered them as patients in the clinic of a German doctor who was a rabid Nazi. It was now March 1939. Fortunately Dr Kung and Bernard Westall came to immediate agreement.

Unlike the Americans, De La Rue asked no guarantees. The company agreed to construct a factory in Shanghai and to print China's notes there; it would also build a second factory in Rangoon which was to operate if the Japanese occupied Shanghai. In return the Chinese Government placed a firm order worth £5 million for the printing of two thousand million notes.

One important proviso was made in the contract. Should it prove impossible to manufacture notes in either Shanghai or Rangoon, the remainder were to be printed in England. This vast undertaking was in addition to the extensive negotiations Westall had concluded with Dr Kung on his London visit in Coronation year. For £25 Avramow bought the only available bottle of French brandy in Chungking to ameliorate the discomforts of the return air journey to Hong Kong. There Westall and Gerry Norman hurriedly conferred on the building of the Shanghai factory.

\*     \*     \*

The last four months of peacetime were a turmoil of activity. In the East the two factories were being built at top speed. Frank Richardson was overseeing activities in Rangoon, and in Shanghai Gerry Norman and his handful of English staff were living through a situation as fantastic as any to face James Bond. The city was entirely surrounded by Japanese, who, although at war with China, had nevertheless to respect the neutrality of Shanghai's International Settlement, where the De La Rue factory was being built in the French Concession.

Norman managed to find an architect and builders, and the whole project was finished within the incredibly short space of six months. Not only was the factory completed but also accommodation for all the Chinese work-hands. So secret was the task of printing China's banknotes under the nose of her enemy that the Company dared not risk the slightest whisper of it leaking out. Once inside the compound the workers were incarcerated. Their living facilities, including a shop, were provided. Fortunately no one ever queried why it was that the employees did not emerge beyond their factory gates.

Ostensibly the plant had been set up to make playing cards for a De La Rue subsidiary called Goodall. Since the Japanese checked all goods coming into the International Concession they would certainly have seized any banknote printing equipment, because they had started their own sponsored note issue. From London the banknote printing machinery was dispatched under cover of playing-card making apparatus to Goodall in Shanghai. The necessary paper was carefully hidden; every ream sent out from Bunhill Row contained fifty sheets of plain paper on top and four-hundred and seventy sheets of banknote paper underneath. The original plates were smuggled in by members of the London staff in their overcoat pockets. Within the year the machines were in operation and the notes were furtively loaded at night on to dust-carts. This was quite an achievement under difficulties which men with twice Gerry Norman's years and experience would have found insurmountable.

When war was declared in September 1939, the firm was already fully extended, staff were called up, while the volume of work continued to increase; of the headaches which hostilities brought to every business, De La Rue's most immediate one was the problem of removing from London all original printing plates, dies and correspondence files essential to the existence of the Company. Bernard Westall greatly feared for the safety of Bunhill Row. If the City were to suffer heavy enemy bombardment it would be miraculous if the conglomeration of De La Rue buildings in EC1 escaped untouched.

Two large houses were bought at Haywards Heath in Sussex. At considerable inconvenience, head office was transferred to Haywards Heath. As it turned out, this early move was extremely important.

In March 1940 Dr Kung sent for Mr Westall to discuss the explosive situation in Shanghai, which was liable to be overrun by the Japanese at any moment. On the way to Chungking he visited Rangoon where, amid local difficulties, Frank Richardson had worked wonders in getting the banknote factory built and operating. Thence by army transport Mr Westall and Avramow flew over the Himalayas via the notorious route known as 'The Hump'. In Chungking the German clinic, together with its Nazi doctor, had been wiped out by Japanese air raids. This time they stayed at the Government Resthouse.

In the event of a successful German attack on France the Chinese had arranged with De La Rue to move all banknote making equipment out of the French concession in Shanghai to

Rangoon. In addition, Westall now made a further arrangement with Dr Kung which proved to be vital. He got him to agree that a new order for the Farmers' Bank should be printed lithographically. This concession was reassuring for De La Rue. Lithographical plant could be set up anywhere, whereas if Bunhill Row were bombed the Company would be rendered incapable of executing the vast China orders by the infinitely more complicated method of copperplate printing. As Dr Kung had now agreed to the use of lithography for the Farmers' Bank notes, if the worst came to the worst he might agree to the orders for the other Chinese banks being produced by the same process.

The Managing Director got back to England a month before the German attack on Holland, Belgium and France. The fall of France was imminent, and in anticipation of the fact that the Japanese would overrun the French settlement in Shanghai, the code-word for the closing of the Shanghai factory was sent out. All the machinery was secretly and safely transferred to Rangoon. In spite of the submarine menace, most of the paper needed by the Rangoon factory got through, and the sinkings of finished Chinese notes from Bunhill Row were minimal – fortunately for De La Rue, who were financially responsible to the Chinese Government for the face value of any notes presented in China. Once some De La Rue notes were washed up off the Galway coast, but to the disappointment of hopeful Irishmen, they were pronounced valueless.

\*     \*     \*

At daybreak on 1st January 1941 the Managing Director was telephoned in Sussex to be told that the London factories were in flames. Hoping against hope that there was a chance of salvaging at least some of them, he could not reach the City fast enough. He arrived to find the burning remnants of Bunhill Row. In that street, the scene of most of De La Rue's life history, several hundred workpeople were already surveying the scene. Many were crying unashamedly. Closely knit by the concerted efforts of the past few years they felt that it was their own house which had been hit.

That very morning Bernard Westall had arranged for a lunch to be given at the Great Eastern Hotel for all foremen and charge-hands. John Caunt, the manager of the Printing Works, came up and took his arm to comfort him. 'Pity our lunch is off, Sir', he added. 'Off', said the Managing Director, 'Tell everyone it's on'.

Using the Great Eastern Hotel as an office, for he now had no other in London, Mr Westall sent off a telegram. It was addressed to Dr Kung in Chungking and it said: 'Factories destroyed by enemy action. Please place additional order for thousand million notes to be printed by lithography'. Considering that the company had barely a factory roof to its head, it was a near-Churchillian gesture. Years of patience with the Chinese Minister of Finance were rewarded. Responding heroically Dr Kung did not hesitate. Back came his telegram: 'Agree'. The situation was saved.

Over lunch at the Great Eastern Hotel the Managing Director made a short speech. He ended: 'Today we have seen the burning ruins of our banknote factories. But it is the factories that have been destroyed – we, not they, are De La Rue. New factories will one day be built, far finer than the ones you have been weeping for this morning. Today is the beginning of a new, and let us hope a better, De La Rue'.

Sure enough the old phoenix rose out of the dust in Bunhill Row and shook his feathers. Thomas's house was indeed rebuilt – how is another story.

# Authorities consulted

If sources are implicit in the text they are not listed again here. Where they are not mentioned here, or in the text, they may be assumed to have been taken from the De La Rue archives.

## CHAPTER I

J. S. BROMLEY
'Channel Islands Privateers in the War of the Spanish Succession', *Transactions of the Guernsey Society*, 1949.

MEMBERS OF THE GUERNSEY SOCIETY
*The Guernsey Farmhouse*, De La Rue, London, 1963.

T. S. ASHTON
*The Industrial Revolution* 1760–1830, Oxford University Press, 1948.

AUGUSTE VACQUERIES
*Profiles et Grimaces*, Michel Levy, Paris, 1856.

ELISHA DOBRÉE
'Diary', *Transactions of the Guernsey Society*, 1929–30.

COLONEL R. T. MARSHAL FRASER
'Printing in the Channel Islands', *Transactions of the Guernsey Society*, 1950.
*Gazette de l'Île de Guernsey* 1812–1814 (*Guernsey Star* archives).
*Miroir Politique* (Priaulx Library, St Peter Port).

ANDRÉ MAUROIS
*Victor Hugo*, Cape, London, 1956.

ALFRED BLACKWELL
(for information about the North Devon Athenaeum).

CHAPTER II

HARRY INWARDS
*Straw Hats, their History and Manufacture*, Pitman, London, 1922.

*The Official Descriptive and Illustrated Catalogue of the Great Exhibition*, Vol. 2. Victoria and Albert Museum, London, 1851.

DR ALAN MUNBY
Kings College, Cambridge
(for information about bookbinding).

RUARI MACLEAN
*Victorian Book Design*, Faber, London, 1963.

R. M. BURCH
*Colour Printing and Colour Printers*, Pitman, London, 1910.

GIDEON MANTELL
*Journal* 1812–1852 ed. Cecil Curwen, Oxford University Press, 1940.

*Cinq Siècles de Cartes à Jouer en France.* (Catalogue of Exhibition in Paris, 1963).

*Chambers' Edinburgh Journal*, 1846.

WESTMINSTER BANK ARCHIVES
(for information about Esdaile's Bank).

CHARLES LAMB
*Essays of Elia* p. 45, Oxford University Press, World's Classics, 1934.

ANDRÉ MAUROIS
*Prometheus, The Life of Balzac*, Bodley Head, London, 1965.

'AN AMATEUR'
*Real Life in London*, Jones and Co., London, 1831.

## AUTHORITIES CONSULTED

E. J. LABARRE
*Dictionary and Encyclopaedia of Paper and Paper-making*, Oxford University Press, 1952.

DARD HUNTER
*Paper-Making; The History and Technique of an Ancient Craft*, Pleiades, London, 1947.

E. B. CHANCELLOR
*Life in Regency and Victorian Times 1800–1850*, Batsford, London, 1927.

JOHN ROBERTS CHANTER
*Literary History of Barnstaple*, Arnold, London, 1866.

MARQUIS DE CUSTINE
*Journey of Our Time* (translated from the French *La Russie en 1839*), Barker, London, 1953.


### CHAPTER III

H. M. CROOME & R. J. HAMMOND
*An Economic History of Britain*, London, Christophers, 1947.

PHILIP CROMPTON, of James R. Crompton Bros. Limited (for information about T. B. Crompton).

B. T. BARTON
*History of Farnworth & Kersley*, De La Rue archives.

WESTMINSTER BANK ARCHIVES
(for information about the failure of Esdaile's Bank, 1837).

MRS C. S. PEEL
'Homes and Habits' in *Early Victorian England* edited by G. M. Young, Vol. I, Oxford University Press, 1934.

'AN AMATEUR'
*Real Life in London*, ibid.

CHAPTER IV

Archives of the College of Ste Barbe, Paris.

R. FLENLEY
*Modern Europe and the World*, Dent, London, 1931.

JOAN EVANS
*The Endless Web, John Dickinson & Co. Ltd*, Cape, London, 1955.

J. GLOAG
*Victorian Taste*, Black, London, 1962.

GEORGE BIRBECK HILL
*The Life of Sir Rowland Hill & the History of Penny Postage*, 2 vols, De La Rue, London, 1880.

*Bradshaw's Journal*, 16th April 1842.

*Chambers' Edinburgh Journal*, 18th July 1846.

CHARLES DICKENS
*Household Words*, Vol. VI, London, 1853.

ELIZABETH LONGFORD
*Victoria R. I.*, Weidenfeld & Nicholson, London, 1964.

SIR DONALD MACKENZIE WALLACE
*Russia*, Cassell, London, 1905.

COL. EION MERRY
(for information about Ross & Walter Winans).

PRINCE DE BEARN ET CHALAIS
(for information about Ross Winans, his great-great-grandfather).
*Monthly Notices of the Royal Astronomical Society*, Vol. I, No. I., 4th February 1890.

WILLIAM ANDREW CHATTO
*Facts & Speculations on the Origin and History of Playing Cards*, Russell Smith, London, 1848.

'CAVENDISH'
*Card Essays*, De La Rue, London, 1879.

## AUTHORITIES CONSULTED

### CHAPTER V

SIR MATTHEW NATHAN
*The Annals of West Coker*, Cambridge University Press, 1957.

MRS C. S. PEEL
*Early Victorian England*, ibid.

GIDEON MANTELL
*Journal*, ibid.

CHRISTOPHER HOBHOUSE
*1851 and the 'Crystal Palace'*, John Murray, London, 1937.

*Illustrated London News*, 1851.

*Morning Herald*, 1851.

*The Official Catalogue of The Great Exhibition*, ibid.

YVONNE FRENCH
*The Great Exhibition*, 1851, Harvill Press, London, 1950.

### CHAPTER VI

JOHN EASTON
*The De La Rue History of British and Foreign Postage Stamps*, Faber, London, 1958.

'CAVENDISH'
*Card Essays*, ibid.

GEORGE BIRBECK HILL
*The Life of Sir Rowland Hill*, ibid.

*Transactions of the Royal Chemical Society*, Vol. XCV, p. 25.

### CHAPTER VII

A. D. MACKENZIE
*The Bank of England Note*, Cambridge University Press, 1953.

ARCHIVES OF HAMBROS BANK
(for letter from Count Cavour to Baron Hambro).

## CHAPTER IX

R. FLENLEY
*Modern Europe and The World,* ibid.

AUGUSTUS DIETZ
*The Postal Service of the Confederate States of America, Richmond, Virginia,* Dietz Printing Company, Richmond, 1929.

*Reports of Cases Argued and Adjudged in the Supreme Court of the U.S., Term* 1865.

## CHAPTER X

The *Art Journal,* 1857.

## CHAPTER XI

EAGLE STAR INSURANCE COMPANY
(for notes on Colonel Billy de la Rue).

## CHAPTER XII

*Rapport sur Mr Warren de la Rue,* 13th December 1880, Archives, Academie des Sciences, Paris.

## CHAPTER XIV

ELIZABETH LONGFORD
*Victoria R. I.,* ibid.

## CHAPTER XV

PHILIP MAGNUS
*King Edward the Seventh,* John Murray, London, 1964.

## CHAPTER XVII

SIDNEY POLLARD
*The Development of the British Economy* 1914–1950, Arnold, London, 1962.

## CHAPTER XIX

Archives of Portals Limited.

AUTHORITIES CONSULTED

CHAPTER XX

HAROLD NICOLSON
*King George V : His Life and Reign,* Constable, London, 1952.


CHAPTER XXIII

H. G. W. WOODHEAD
*Adventures in Far Eastern Journalism,* Hokuseido Press, Tokyo, 1935.

# INDEX